The glory of

MCMLXXXI

Elsevier - Amsterdam / Brussels

AMSTERDAM

Idea and Photography: A. van der Heyden

Text: Ben Kroon / Ton Land

Contents

Foreword

The Glory of Amsterdam is a personal impression of the chief characteristics of the country's capital. It is not by any means intended to be a complete inventory. For this, twice the number of pages would be needed, if not more.
It does seek to encourage visitors and inhabitants alike to look about them and discover what Holland and Amsterdam have to offer in the way of beauty and heirlooms from the distant and the not-so-distant past. Another aim of this book is to foster a less wasteful attitude towards a physical environment that – certainly in a city the size of Amsterdam – must be considered a rare and invaluable patrimony.

Page 1: central portion of a house with a neck gable on the Kloveniersburgwal (no. 62). Pages 2-3: view over the Reguliersgracht towards the Thorbeckeplein. Page 4: View from the St. Anthonie Lock towards the Montelbaanstoren.

© MCMLXXXI Elsevier Publishing Projects S.A., Lausanne
D/MCMLXXXI/0199/259   ISBN 90 10 037916
Layout and production: Frits Vesters
Typesetting: Damman Typography, Amsterdam
Lithography: Art Color Offset, Rome
Printing: Boom Ruygrok b.v., offset Haarlem
Binding: Stokkink b.v., Amsterdam.

The coat of arms of Amsterdam

1

2

Built in 1638, the old Excise Office (3) in the Oudebrugsteeg displays the complete coat of arms of Amsterdam, with three St. Andrew's crosses, two lions and the crown of the Holy Roman Emperor Maximilian I. If you look carefully, you can see the city's coat of arms in many places, for example on the University Library (2), over the entrance to the Lending Bank (4), on an 'ordinary' house on Kromme Waal (1) and over the entrance to the City Orphanage in the Kalverstraat (5). Particularly common on public buildings, charitable institutions and city gates, it is found with all sorts of variations but almost always includes the imperial crown, which continued to be a source of pride even in the Republic. After the Second World War, in 1946, Queen Wilhelmina added the motto *Heroic, Resolute, Charitable* in recognition of the capital's conduct during the occupation. The history of the city's coat of arms can be traced back to the early 15th century.

The coat of arms of Amsterdam
1 Kromme Waal 17. 2 University
Library, Singel. 3 Excise House,
Oudebrugsteeg. 4 Lending Bank,
Oudezijds Voorburgwal. 5 Historical
Museum, Kalverstraat 92.

3

4

A seal of Amsterdam dating from 1416 shows two men in a cockboat flying the city banner with three St. Andrew's crosses. St. Andrew's crosses are shaped like the letter X and derive their name from the tradition that St. Andrew was crucified on such a cross. It is not known with certainty how they came to be adopted for the city's coat of arms, but it is thought that the banner originated with the Lords of Amstelland. Also known as the Lords of Persijn, these predecessors of the Lords of Amstel took part in the Crusades and probably chose the St. Andrew's cross for their armorial bearings while they were in the Holy Land. The city's coat of arms occurs in its oldest form on the Excise House, which was built in 1638 by Jacob van Campen and used by the collectors of import duties on commodities such as grain, beer and fuel. The right to adorn the coat of arms with the imperial crown was granted by Maximilian in 1489. The highest crown in Amsterdam is that on top of the 85-metre-high Westertoren (West Tower), silhouetted against the sky.

One of the most beautiful coats of arms is to be found in the Kalverstraat above the gateway of what was once the City Orphanage and is now the Historical Museum. Aside from the many interesting features of the gate itself, the use of yellow paving stones in the small forecourt makes this one of the few places where a by-law dating from 1672 is still complied with. The by-law required that public thoroughfares be paved with yellow stones for the greater convenience of people using them at night. The yellow paving of the Kalverstraat leads to the gateway, a fine example of the Renaissance style built in 1581 by Joost Jansz. Bilhamer, who also designed the Oude Kerk (Old Church) tower. The relief above the arch shows a group of orphans gathered around a dove symbolizing the Holy Ghost. As the children's clothes are in the city's colours – white, black and red – the work combines strikingly with the majestic, festoon-framed coat of arms on the upper part of the wall.

The gateway has also enriched the Dutch language by giving it the famous and oft-quoted lines by Vondel inscribed under the relief: *Wij groeien vast in tal en last/Ons tweede Vaders klagen* (We are growing steadily in number and burden/Our second Fathers complain).

Two less famous lines on a second relief urged the passer-by to support the institution:

Ay ga niet voort door deze poort
Of help het luttel dragen
(Pass not through this gate/Without helping the little ones).

5

Gateway to the city

building that rose from gate to weigh-house is that it was used by numerous guilds. The reliefs and texts above the doors form a permanent reminder that masons, surgeons, civic guards and others held their meetings there.

A great many famous men and artists of all kinds have entered the Waag (Weigh House) through the doorway of the Guild of St. Luke, which still survives. The guild had such a wide range of members – from painters of pictures to painters of houses, from stonemasons, statue-founders and smiths to printers and booksellers – that its meetings were regularly attended by men such as Hendrick de Keyser, Quellinus, Verhulst and Rembrandt. In the round tower room belonging to the Surgeons' Guild (the words 'Theatrum Anatomicum' are still displayed above this guild's entrance) Rembrandt painted 'The Anatomy Lesson of Dr. Nicolaes Tulp', and later 'The Anatomical Lesson of Dr. Jean Deyman', which was partially destroyed by fire in 1723. The surviving portion can be seen in the Rijks-museum.

The Waag came very close to being pulled down in 1829, when it became one of a long list of monuments scheduled for demolition. The people who saved it from undergoing the same fate as the Haringpakkerstoren (Herring Packers Tower) and the Jan Roodenpoortstoren on the Singel were the surgeons, who managed to persuade the municipal authorities that the building was indispensable for their work. Anatomy continued to be taught in the Waag until 1869.

6 The towers of the former Anthonies-poort. 7 Loophole in one of the towers.

Amsterdam's real gates have disappeared. In the earliest phase of its history, Amsterdam had neither gates nor walls. Such enemies as there may have been at that time could apparently be kept out without difficulty.

In the 15th century, however, a wall was built around the city to meet the challenge of new and more destructive weapons. One of the main fortified gates was constructed at the junction of the Zeedijk and the Anthoniesdijk and probably incorporated an already existing gate. The Anthoniespoort (6) in the Nieuwmarkt (New Market) is the only gate that has been preserved from the original wall. There are few buildings in the city that can be dated with such exactness, for an inscription carved by the builders on a stone that is still in place tells us – freely translated – 'The first stone of this gate was laid on April 28, 1488'. The six smaller towers date from this

period; the large tower was added in 1692. The towers are round at the bottom, octagonal at the top. Still to be seen are corbels with carvings of men's heads which, though not master-pieces, are undeniably charming.

The original gate was lapped by water, but when the Kloveniers-burgwal was partially drained in 1614 it was left high and dry in a large field, in which the Sint Anthonies-markt was later held. Fortunately, after the extension of 1614 had brought the gate inside the city, Amsterdam's governors saw a way of putting it to use: they decreed 'that the old St. Anthoniespoort shall be converted into a weigh-house'. The walls were raised, the inner court was covered and scales were set up under awnings in front of the four small entrances. The chief things weighed there were anchors, guns and the like. Another reason for the survival of this

No Roman ruins..., an introduction

By European standards, Amsterdam is not an ancient city. Her history does not stretch beyond the thirteenth century. The first mention of people living by the dam on the river Amstel was found in a 1275 charter; that is why the city celebrated its 700th anniversary in 1975. No Roman ruins, no reminders of Charlemagne, no romanesque churches, not even a cathedral – in the Middle Ages Amsterdam had to bow to other towns in the region. The bishop lived in Haarlem and even the ancient privilege of providing the executioner fell to that city. The tremendous prosperity of the seventeenth century made Amsterdam the country's capital, following the independance of the Republic; even this honourable title is disputable as it was never written down in the constitution. The government has its seat in The Hague and the former Queen had her residence in Soestdijk. Amsterdam is the capital because 'that is where things happen', a city with initiative, not only in commerce but in all spheres of life. It is a city which is frequently in the news and which, in a typical Dutch love-hate relationship, is criticised, loved and admired, as *prima inter pares*. And literally so, as the Netherlands, and particularly the densely-populated western provinces, is almost one big city. Nowhere are the towns so close together, even in the Middle Ages, each with their own walls, their own form of government and their own style. No strict central authority with impressive buildings and an aristocratic court has ever had the chance to spread its influence.

The old republic was a citizen's republic and Amsterdam is the capital of a citizen's country. If you look westwards from the Dam you can see the imposing façade of a big seventeenth-century building – it used to be the town hall but is now the Palace. It only changed its function a hundred and fifty years ago, during the French occupation when the town councillor from Orange was elevated to the rank of constitutional monarch – and Holland had a king. Amsterdam offered its town hall to the king as a royal residence, a decision which many Amsterdammers regret, to this very day. There are many who maintain that the transaction should be declared invalid so that the building can be used by the city councillors once more, and especially so that the bronze doors can be opened again that every citizen may be free to go in and walk round in the city's 'best' room – the Burgerzaal (Civic Hall).

In the shadow of the palace/town hall stands a modest mediaeval building without towers – the Nieuwe Kerk (New Church). The church plays an important part in national life as every new monarch is inaugurated there in the presence of the States General. But members of the House of Orange are buried elsewhere – in Delft. The Nieuwe Kerk is not a royal church but really an old city church: the church has never played a dominant part in Amsterdam. No bishop's palace can be found in the city, and a 17th century plan to embellish the church with a high tower was rejected by the mayors as they preferred to spend the money on the completion of the town hall. But Amsterdam is rife with churches of all sorts and sects. The citizens thought that tolerance and spiritual freedom were more important than unity.

The foundations in Amsterdam were not strong enough to support the spread of power of a monarchy or a church. At the opening of the town hall on 19th January 1657 the first two lines of a poem by Constantijn Huygens were read: 'Illustrious founders of the world's eighth wonder. As much stone above as wood beneath'. These lines are significant. Huygens calls the town hall 'the Eighth Wonder of the World'. That was not simply a mutual compliment to those who knew their classics, but also an allusion to the immense pride of the little republic – an exception among the absolute monarchies of Europe – this republic, and particularly the merchant town of Amsterdam, had risen to become the most important commercial centre in the world. For its governors, the commercial metropolis had built the biggest and, in many respects, the most costly civic building of the seventeenth century.

But the second line is even more interesting, 'as much stone above as wood beneath' – the stones were heavy blocks which had been dragged from far afield. Nowhere on Dutch soil is natural stone to be found; building was a matter of wood and brick.

The clay from the rivers, fired to a manageable size, was the best building material. The mayors only wanted stone houses to measure up to their rivals in southern lands. But that huge, heavy stone would have sunk away in the mud if deep foundations had not been built on piles – and that is 'as much wood beneath'.

Every Dutch school child knows that the Palace/Town Hall is built on 13,659 piles – invisible piles. The whole of Amsterdam is built on piles. If one could make an 'x-ray' photo of the city, a marvellous picture would be revealed: a jungle of piles, which stretch down through the muddy peat and ground water to the first or second layer of sand, the real foundation of the city. A city in a marsh, an embanked river, by an inlet in the sea, a water-city. The water was both friend and foe. The effort of building a city in such an unfavourable place was rewarded by the fact that water brought wealth. In the Europe of these days with its bad roads, water was the only way to carry goods safely and quickly from one place to another. Whoever had water at his doorstep had a chance to become rich. And Amsterdam was not only situated on the waterside but also centrally, on the old freight route from the south to the north and the east. Initially this route followed the safe inland water-ways, but later when the ships increased in size and the navigation techniques became more reliable, the route went by the sea.

From the tumult which accompanied the vast expansions in Europe, in the wake of the voyages of discovery and the wars that crippled and impoverished the great powers, the Republic emerged for the first time at the beginning of the seventeenth century. The Netherlands became Europe's freight carrier and tranport centre. Adventurers who dared to take on long voyages streamed in from small towns and villages. Years later the ships returned, sometimes with only a quarter of the original crew but mostly with a sufficiently valuable cargo to satisfy their patrons and encourage them to finance still more ships.

By our standards, the period of expansion and adventure was incredibly hard. Prosperity was literally culled from every corner of the world and Amsterdam grew faster than ever. Very quickly, the city numbered 200,000 inhabitants which in those days made it a busy metropolis, an international centre, which could only cope with the increasing industry by attracting immigrants to build and crew the ships.

Money was poured into ships and cargos, and there was also money for the expansion of the city. What is now the most characteristic part of Amsterdam – the old centre ringed by canals – was probably conceived, not by a famous artist but by an official surveyor, who stuck the compass on the Dam and drew a semi-circle round the mediaeval city. Experts cannot agree on who should be credited with the design. Perhaps no one gave it much thought then; the city was rapidly growing and building had to keep pace.

The plan to multiply the size of the city was systematically followed. In the west, the city was extended and built up with three broad canals – the Herengracht (Gentlemen's Canal), the Keizersgracht (Emperors' Canal) and the Prinsengracht (Princes' Canal) – as well as smaller canals and streets leading to the centre. At first this development only went halfway round the circle, as far as the Leidsegracht, but as the expansion continued so the compass drew the full circle, over the Amstel and back to the water front. A defence dyke was built around this, with 26 windmills at strategic points – even the wind was put

8 Amsterdam inside its medieval walls, painted by J. Merker in 1684 but probably based on the work by Cornelis Anthonisz dating from a century and a half earlier. The painting shows a city abounding in water.

9 View of the Amstel from the Hoge Sluis with part of the picture evoked by Vondel's words: 'She who carries the crown of Europe as an empress opens out magnificently on the Amstel and on the IJ'. A new town hall is to be built on the site occupied by the houses in the background, which have since been demolished.

to good use. In the west the circle was drawn more amply and between the canals and the defence wall, the town's craftsmen settled and the area soon became known as the Jordaan. Where this name came from is still a subject of discussion and there is probably no single answer.

The Jordaan did not have the grandeur of the canals; it was an area with small streets and straight narrow canals – in fact, quite functional and not romantic. It became the first working-class area in the city, with its own way of life, friendly and lively – just as it is today.

It was no coincidence that Amsterdam grew so systematically. If the town had been built on more solid ground then its growth would have taken place in the same disorderly fashion as it did everywhere else in Euope. But in a marshland area it is only possible to build if the drainage is perfected and the land raised. The Dutch word 'gracht' (canal) comes from 'graven' (to dig).

With such rapid expansion it was in the interests of the city to build systematically. The traditional care, which Amsterdam has always taken in town-planning – despite a decline in the century – finds its origin in the soil. The authorities are really the only ones who can organise the extensive preparation and almost automatically they are the ones who control the distribution of land.

In practice this meant that equal-sized plots of land along the canals were measured out and sold to builders. The imposing rhythm of the canals with the carefully balanced harmony of their proportions finds its source in a few simple standard measurements. The places where that rhythm was later disrupted, are immediately apparent. Fortunately, that has not occurred very frequently. Once the canals were completed, they gave the Amsterdammers reason to be proud. They sensed that great work had been done. You can walk along along the canals for hours without feeling bored. They may stretch for miles, but they are never dull, the bends always reveal another part of the picture.

It is even more striking to take the boat and look at the canals from the water. In fact, the same picture repeats itself: tall, narrow houses with elegant clock gables alternating with extra wide houses with frame gables, a high canal wall, the street in front of the houses and especially the trees, which in Amsterdam are usually elms. There is a painting preserved of the 'new' canals without trees; it gives a very bare impression. Trees bring nature to this townscape, the rhythm of the seasons – in the winter the gables show through clearly, in the summer the buildings are blurred behind a green screen.

There is a striking absence of big squares and public buildings. There are only a few places where the picture opens out, such as by the Westerkerk (West Church), with its high tower topped with a colourful crown in memory of the one Emperor Maximilian of Austria gave to the city's coat of arms in 1489 and which has always been held in honour. The city councillors in 1620 may have been republicans but they demonstrated their pride in this gift by placing a crown on the highest tower of the city.

Every house on the canal had, and still has, its garden at the back. Public parks and gardens are not a part of the old city. Every canal-house owner had his own garden which he looked after with care. Between the richest canals runs a narrow street where the coach-houses were built. A real patrician's house usually comprised two plots. At the front, the canalside, it had an elegant gable and a flight of steps. At the back, there was a room looking out over the lawn and summer house which was sometimes decorated and stood back-to-back with the coach-house with its doors on the back street. That is how the merchants lived, whose wealth often greatly exceeded that of other European noblemen. They did not live like princes but as citizens, hundreds of them, side by side along the same canal, without magnificent courtyards or drives. The office, and sometimes even the storeroom, were also part of the same house, certainly in the beginning when the merchant was still building up a capital. Later, when prosperity was assured and the wealthy organised the distribution of the most profitable positions, especially that of mayor, ostentation became more refined. The canal house became the town house, the family residence, but in the summer the merchants went to the country, to a huge mansion on the River Vecht or on the edge of the dunes. These people plumed themselves with magnificent ancient names or adopted a noble title from impoverished German princes who came to Holland to borrow money. That was the eighteenth century, the rococo period, the elegant era, when the French fashion was dominant and many canal houses were converted according to the new trend. Whoever visits a patrician's house today will almost always find an interior that is a century younger than the exterior. Successive generations have tried to make their mark and this has resulted in a picture strangely varied but nonetheless harmonious because people were bound by the original size of the plots. Even within these limitations many hundreds of variations were possible: rich gables in the style of the 'Dutch renaissance', using orange bricks and white stone, with ornamentation and arabesques, festive, extrovert façade and next to them strictly calculated stone façades with a few cool accents, very aloof; these patricians' houses stand side by side, without letting each other down, very tolerant, citizens with a healthy selfrespect, façades with an individual coutenenance. We have already mentioned that there are scarcely any squares within the circle of canals; in fact they are almost totally absent from the city. There were only squares by the city gates so that the horses could be unharnessed. Goods travelled by water; that was cheaper and easier. Squares demanded valuable space and, moreover, in such a wet and windy climate, they were not nice places to stop. There were markets on the canal side of the streets; every article had a special place. Only the important goods, the real merchandise like grain, were sold in a separate building. Of course, for the most important transactions there was the Exchange which was built as a bridge over the Amstel by the Dam - the seventeenth century dam in the river bed that gave the city its name. There would be many more such interventions in nature.

Amsterdam's third produce exchange, built in 1903

1   2   3   4

by Berlage and recognised throughout the world as an architectural innovation, also stands on a filled-in canal and gives the city councillors reason for concern as the unstable subsoil causes cracks in the building. Whoever drives through those Amsterdam streets which by modern standards are relatively broad, can be almost sure that he is on a canal that was filled in during the last century. The street names themselves reveal those streets that were by chance somewhat wider, for instance the Reguliersbreestraat ('bree' means 'broad'). However, the wide avenue which is the Damrak came into existence by filling in part of the oldest harbour, the mouth of the Amstel, of which only a narrow canal remains. In the old days, the houses and warehouses stood on either side of the Damrak (Dam Straight) in the water which was full of moored ships from the river mouth to the Dam. The broad Rokin was also built on the old riverbed on the other side of the Dam, where the 'straight' began. The wide Nieuwezijds Voorburgwal, the Spuistraat and the Spui (sluice) were all once canals. If you can imagine that the street is no longer there and the water is back, you will realise that the proportions are much better. And if you cannot do that, you can see paintings of old Amsterdam in the Historical Museum; these paintings seem sometimes sad as the original situation was so much more harmonious. The broad avenue which is the Raadhuisstraat and its prolongation, the Rozengracht, break a path across the ring of canals – another filled-in waterway. The broad Vijzelstraat was originally as narrow as the Leidsestraat or Utrechtsestraat, but it was completely demolished and widened on one side. The buildings on the side which was demolished are in proportion with the broad boulevard, whereas the other side of course is still related to the original situation.

In the Jordaan many canals were filled in, not to mention the recent changes made in what used to be the Jodenbuurt (the Jewish Quarter). One can regret this, but it is fortunate that the delicate pattern of the waterways has not been spoilt more radically. This might easily have occurred in the last century when

Development of the gables in Amsterdam

A ridged roof logically ends in a gable. In the Middle Ages, when wood was in general use for house building, the most common type (1) had coupled windows and a king post, while the gable was framed by a strip of wood along each side to close off the thatched roof.
In Amsterdam as in other cities, the frequency of major fires led to the passing of by-laws intended to encourage the use of brick. The by-law that finally brought about the demise of the wooden gable in Amsterdam was passed in 1669. Outside the cities, however, the tradition survived into the 19th century.
The least elaborate type of brick gable is the so called spout gable (2), which is found in Amsterdam particularly in back gables and warehouses. Also dating from the Middle Ages is the step gable (3), technically and aesthetically one of the most satisfactory ways of leading horizontal brick courses to a point. The pilaster in the upper part of the gable is reminiscent of the king post in wooden gables. Scrollwork, in which convoluted ribands were joined to form tracery and frames, was a popular type of decoration in the Renaissance and was also applied to gables. A similar profile could be achieved in step gables by the use of side-pieces (4).
The ever more dominant part played by ornamentation in the late Renaissance gave rise to the neck gable, or Vingboons gable (5 and 6). Neck gables with a stepped profile reminiscent of phase 4 are known as 'elevated' neck gables (5). The fusion of form and ornament achieved in the bell gable (7) explains its still being in favour in the 18th century, the age of the Rococo. A remarkable variant is the ogee bell gable (8).

5   6   7   8

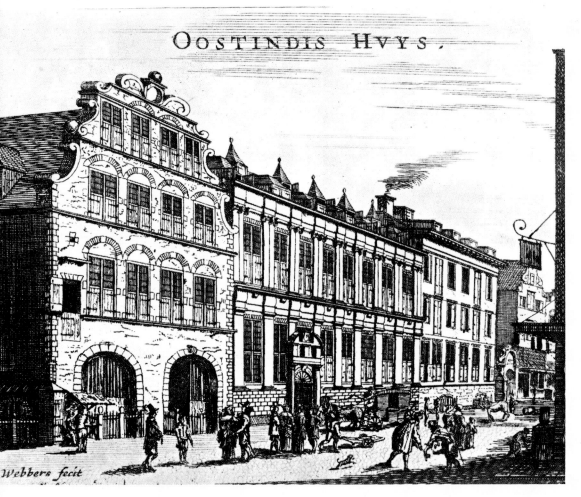

OOSTINDIS HVYS,

Webbers fecit

10 A glimpse of 16th century Amsterdam: 'Het Oostindisch Huis' (East India House) in the Oude Hoogstraat. The old part was the Bushuis, on the left, which was built c. 1550, used for storing spices from 1603 onwards and demolished in 1890. The rest of the complex, arranged around a courtyard, was added in the course of the 17th century.

there was a population explosion and within a few generations the population had quadrupled.

This growth reached a climax in the period of industralisation, and of road and rail traffic which made completely different demands on the city than in the two preceding centuries.

It has already been mentioned that the Historical Museum houses a rich collection of views of the old city. Amsterdam is one of the most frequently portrayed cities in Europe. Scarcely has any city been so often mapped and painted. That is also related to the character of the city's inhabitants. Nine hundred maps of the old city alone have been preserved; there are some in which every house is realistically drawn. Maps of many foreign capitals show a vast complex of courtyards and broad avenues, with the rest of the town vaguely sketched in, but maps of Amsterdam showed individual life and character in every little corner. This was the thing that amazed foreign visitors most, even in the old days; the great sense of self-respect that people had, the feeling of being lord and master in one's own home, on one's own land, in one's own city – and not having to kneel to anyone. That feeling gave rise to the thousands of expressive façades. Let us take a look at one. A tall, narrow building, part of a row, on street-level, or flight of

steps, perhaps simple but always well-proportioned, occasionally elaborate and stylish with beautiful carving, craftsmanship which is frequently to be found in details. That was seldom the work of well-known artists, the craftsman who undertook that task took care of the design. He was affiliated to a guild and if he wanted to become a full member, he had to give proof of his capabilities. Design and execution came from the same hand. The steps lead to the door which is also frequently a special design, for example with two sections so that the top half can be opened on summerly days. At the top of the steps there is often a seat, where the house-owner could sit – in those days there were no balconies. We can see this in the paintings of the time – the inhabitants sitting there in comfortable gown, smoking a pipe – a jovial picture.

Later people became more elegant and did not appear like that any more. Above the door there is a window, with an ornament, sometimes with the owner's initials or a symbolic design.

The façade is made of small bricks, carefully laid and minutely pointed, exemplary building, as building was a craft too. What a masterbuilder had to accomplish before he was accepted in the guild can be seen in the Waag (Weigh House) on the Nieuwmarkt where many masterworks have been preserved. Looking at them, one is overawed by so much craftsmanship. The fame of the canal houses has not come by chance; it is attributable to the sturdy basis of craftsmanship in every branch of the building industry that was highly honoured. The construction of a house was a costly business. When walking through the old centre one cannot forget that is was built by some of the richest people in the world. It is no average place. The quantity deserves special mention, the huge number of houses and the whole gamut of palatial residences which were houses for the ordinary man, each one with its own character, always carefully and imaginatively built, never thoughtless or slipshod; the wealth of the city was not restricted to a few hands but was distributed among many. The eyes travel up the façade to the top of the gable.

The middle of the gable is in the shape of the front of a clock decorated with stones. The decorations were made according to the fashion of the day; a connoisseur would be able to date them because despite their variations, they are all based on a particular pattern. A clock gable, a neck gable with ornamental side-pieces, a spout gable, a step gable, an elevated neck gable, a frame gable, and so on; they have been named and classified but there are no two alike. Every house has its own face. Sometimes you can see a gable stone; there are a many hundreds in Amsterdam. They gave the house a name and this name was frequently based on the place of birth, the profession or a particular occurrence in the life of the owner. Sometimes they were based on a religious saying, or on a joke, a riddle, a lamentation, a biblical scene, an example of traditional art or folk wisdom, – all of these are the delight of the enthusiast, and some have even earned a place in a museum.

There is yet another striking detail in a gable: the everpresent hoisting beam which, though it reminds us that the attics were used as storerooms, is still part of life today. Goods were brought by water, and hoisted up to the attic with a windlass; this was an installation, common to every house or warehouse, with a wooden shaft by the attic window and a rope that reached to the ground where it could be operated. An ingenious piece of equipment but nothing special in a city where everyone was used to working with wood – after all hundreds of ships and windmills had been built there; it was a world of inventors, just like the America of the last century.

The hoisting beams only come into their own for removals nowadays. In those days, even such a simple part of a house had to be given some individuality. Sometimes very amusing, such as on the Prins Hendrikkade where the mechanism is hidden in a lion's head.

As the proprietor prospered, so the decoration on his gable flourished. Sometimes you can see circular windows at the top of the house, framed with elegant stones. An 'oeil-de-boeuf', garlands, flowers and fruit of stone beneath windows or added to the brickwork. The harmony is what strikes one, even in the most intricate gables. The well-known complaint that in the old days they just could not build ugly things – sounds more secretive than it is. Measuring and fitting was based on good proportions, the perfect cut and all its variations. No profession is so bound by traditions as the building profession, and in those days the skills were passed down from master to apprentice. And that was what the householder expected. An unbalanced gable would have been as unthinkable as a windmill without sails. People had an image of what at a house should be, in the same way as they

11 Façades on the Keizersgracht with (left) the 'Huis met de hoofden' (House with Heads).

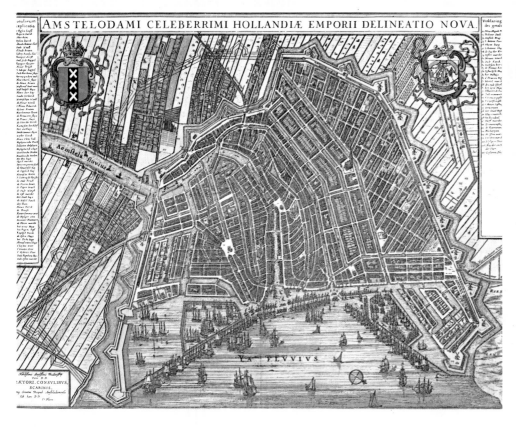

AMSTELODAMI CELEBERRIMI HOLLANDIÆ EMPORII DELINEATIO NOVA.

13 Map of Amsterdam made in 1649 by Joan Blaeu with the help of a map produced ten years previously by Hendrik Hondius. The first phase of the great extension which began in 1612 and was to give Amsterdam its characteristic crescent shape was virtually complete in 1649. The city preserved its crescent shape until the mid-19th century, when new districts began to grow up beyond the Singelgracht. The map is included in the book 'Toonneel der steden van de Verenighde Nederlanden met hare beschrijvingen', of part of which a facsimile has been published.

anatomy. They twice commissioned Rembrandt to paint them; the first version is on exhibition in the Mauritshuis in The Hague, and the second, damaged by fire, is in the Rijksmuseum. In those days it was customary to have oneself painted, in groups or singly. Amsterdam has a marvellous collection of Guild Officials. Some are on exhibition in the Rijksmuseum; others are in the Schuttersgalerij (Soldier's Gallery) of the Historical Museum where they are uniquely exhibited in a public street, which is covered and guarded. Much has been preserved from that period but what was perhaps the most vital part has disappeared: the huge fleet of ships in which the Amsterdammers sailed the world's seas. The route to the Baltic, the route to the Levant, to the East and the West Indies, the whale hunt; everywhere where a cargo was to be found and trading was possible, they pressed their way in, often by force of arms. The struggle for power was fought especially with the English, and this led to many wars.

In the Rijksmuseum, there is a huge canvas, painted by Jan van de Velde, showing the city and the IJ with all its ships. This is a realistic view as a register kept in other port proves how large the Dutch – and Amsterdam's – expansion was in this area.

Not one of those ships has been preserved. The Amsterdammers were not sentimental; they only wanted their ships to be preserved in paintings. As for the ships themselves, we are still hoping for one to be discovered on the sea bed, a well-preserved wreck,

a modest compensation for the gap which becomes obvious after a visit to the new Maritime Museum. It has found a new home in the huge old Admirality building that was previously used as a warehouse for equiping the old warships, the country's shipyard, that possesses the largest and most impressive collection of old ships.

One modest monument, connected with shipping, is worth special attention; that is the little tower on the mediaeval town wall which has been preserved on what is now the Prins Hendrikkade. Standing there now, you have to use your imagination because at the end of the last century an island was made in the IJ where the Central Station now stands with the wide railway track leading to it. The old waterfront has become an inner quayside, much to the sorrow of many Amsterdammers. There is however an old Dutch saying that when the tide rises you must move the buoys, that means that if rail transport begins to get the upper hand, then a transport centre such as Amsterdam must adapt itself. It could have been done more elegantly but from the point of view of town planning, it was quite reasonable to build a station where once the fleet had its mooring place – the city was still directed towards the sea. The thousands of tourists, commuters and businessmen who walk from the station into the city each day via the Damrak, follow the same path as the those who entered the city by boat in the old days.

That was the normal means of transport then when

it was no exception for an Amsterdammer to sail
to Petersburg, London, Lisbon or Naples. Or even
further, to the Cape of Good Hope, the East Indies or
to the colony in America, then called New Amsterdam
but rebaptised New York when it fell to the English.

The Schreierstoren (Weeping Tower) has a very old
gable stone in it portraying a woman and child
tearfully waving to a ship.
Thousands and thousands of sailors lost their lives
at sea, an appalling number, but there is scarcely a
single witness to this tragedy. That is surprising, and
only the lachrimose nineteenth century discovered
this theme. The little stone in the tower is the only
souvenir from those unsentimental years. Unsentimental but not insensitive people.
The wealth in the Republic was certainly better distributed than in those countries where the nobility
took all the profits, but nonetheless there was poverty.

Poverty among the Dutch but even more among
immigrant Germans who had fled after the Thirty
Years War. They frequently fell into the hands of
rough recruiters, who were looking for people to do
the dirty work on board ship.
For that sort of poverty no answer had yet been
found. People were very dependent on the charity
of the rich. There was poor relief and some care for
old people, widows and orphans. There was great
rejoicing whenever a wealthy man donated some
money for the building of a home or an almshouse.
The wealthy donator, often a woman, was praised in
golden lettering on the gable.

*14 The Nieuwe Kerk and the town hall, seen from the rear.
This painting by Isaac Ouwater (1748-1793) shows the
foundation of the tower which, though extensive piling was
done, was never built.*

The results are still to be seen in the city, especially in the almshouses, cloistered little dwellings, usually grouped around a garden, with a regal hall for the governors whose portraits also embellished the walls. Almshouses were rentfree, with light and water and sometimes even with free clothes. Every denomination owned a few; some families had established their own to house their older servants. Quiet, intimate places, which have mostly been well-preserved and are now remarkably popular again as quiet retreats in a noisy modern city.

The most beautiful example is the Begijnhof in the heart of the city. It dates from the earliest days of the city's existence and served as a home for devoted women who could live there relatively independently. With the Alteration in 1578, this very Orthodox Catholic centre, unlike the monasteries, was not taken over by the authorities and given a new function.

According to public opinions, this was prevented because some of the inhabitants were related to the elders of the reformed church who were afraid of internal strife.

People assumed that the almshouse inhabitants would gradually die off, but the families survived until a few years ago, when the last inhabitant of the Begijnhof exchanged the temporal for the eternal. The church was, however, taken from the Roman Catholics and given to the Anglicans. But the Begijnhof Catholics soon built a clandestine church in a few houses and the situation has remained unchanged to this day. The Begijnhof is a sanctuary of quiet beauty in the busiest part of the city. It includes the oldest house in the city which is built entirely of wood. Inside many of the almshouses, fragments of mediaeval buildings have been found. A subdued female world in which the Deacon of Amsterdam was the only male inhabitant. In the clandestine church one of the oldest traditions of the city is kept alive, the celebration of the 'Sacrament of the Miracle', the appearance of the Holy Ghost in 1345 that made Amsterdam a place of pilgrimage, culminating in the great Miracle procession that wound its way through the whole city. This tradition reappeared in a completely different form at the end of the last century; a nocturnal trek along the old prilgrim's road, the Peaceful Pageant, a completely silent procession of thousands who walked through the old parts of the city, praying inwardly, a typical form of Dutch devoutness. This was often practised voluntarily in Amsterdam during the most difficult times of the German occupation.

The Peaceful Procession on 4th May, in memory of the dead on the eve of the liberation, found its inspiration in this Peaceful Pageant.

We can see that every group has made its own mark on Amsterdam. The Jews have seen very many words in their language become common usage in Amsterdam. They also gave Amsterdam its nickname: Mokum – 'the only place'. A place for many – traditionally the Amsterdammer is well-known for his tolerance, for the right to individual freedom, an age-old tradition in town and country, which has repeatedly enabled the city to survive social crises without scars and unnecessary victims. Tolerance implies a risk of weakness and dullness. That purposeful avoidance of majesty and that cultivation of detail may seem niggling to many foreigners; they see no vitality, no big movements, just continual elaboration on one theme: coordination instead of subjugation. But that is the superficial repercussion of an attitude, an attitude which has created a marvellous diversity in housing. Not magnificent cathedrals, no palaces, no vast boulevards, no dramatic display of power, but curves, nuances and detail. The vivid intimacy of the Dutch houses can be seen in the paintings of Johannes Vermeer and Pieter de Hoogh, cool poetry vibrant with quiet life, and that indefinable 'cosiness'. The Amsterdammer is a typical Dutchman from the big city, not an easy-going person if you interfere with his personal rights but friendly if you treat him kindly. Very helpful, not afraid to say what he thinks, not chicken-hearted. Above all, he is curious, not refined in his manners yet not really clumsy, preferring to be his own boss, a tradesman rather than an industrial worker. That is inherited from the old merchant city. Amsterdammers can 'fix' things, make compromises together, between bright lads of the same ilk. They know about give and take, are used to foreigners and enjoy travelling themselves. In the summer months you can find them in all corners of Europe. They are sentimental in their belief that life was better in the old days. No one can get that out of an Amsterdammer's head. An old part of the town that has to be demolished arouses not satisfaction but sadness, which explains why preservation plans take root faster in Amsterdam than anywhere else. If there is a chance that the last example of something may disappear altogether, they demand preservation. The last windmill, the last secret church, every time they jump into the breach, and in this way Amsterdam has acquired the largest and most diverse collection of museums in the whole country. Art and artistry thrive in this atmosphere; the art trade is extensive and there is a very intense artistic life.

In the current revival of the threatened cultural life of the city – essential after the exodus of so many people to the middle-class suburbs which left a certain lifelessness in the old parts of the city – Amsterdam makes itself clearly heard. It is a city of many action groups and local committees. Sometimes a difficult city, unpredictable, capricious, with an almost southern temperament, its fire has not yet burnt itself out – one of the most surprising patterns in the richly chequered tapestry of the Europe of yesteryear.

15

The glory of
AMSTERDAM

And there is the city in its early days on a gable stone (18) in the St. Luciënsteeg. Safe within the city walls, the towers rising above them, houses, warehouses, people. The tower of the Oude Kerk (Old Church) (16) in all its glory, warehouses in abundance (17). And the people of those days, inhabitants of a rapidly growing merchant city, busily engaged in all sorts of trades (19-22). The craftsman, the ordinary man, the milkmaid and the corn-porter, who carried one of the most important items of trade – corn from the Baltic countries – from the ships to the warehouses.

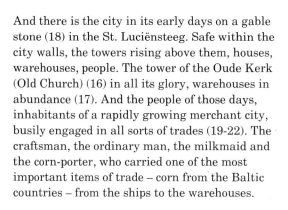

16

17

19

15 Captain Boom with his company before Zwolle – Historical Museum. 16 Spire of the Oude Kerk. 17 Warehouse, 349 Prinsengracht. 18 Gable stone with a view of Amsterdam, St. Luciënsteeg. 19-21 Gable stone portraying inhabitants of Amsterdam: 19 on 295 Spuistraat, the others in the St. Luciënsteeg.

DE·OVDE·SCHANS

18

20

21

22

N

23

D·IONGE·KOOPER·SLAGER

24

Amsterdam's former inhabitants are portrayed in abundance on gable stones, some of them working, others posing. Amsterdam was a crowded city, bustling with activity. Among the more remarkable gable stones is one which shows a young coppersmith working on a large kettle and manages to give the impression that his assistant is in the kettle rather than behind it (23). Several theories have been put forward to explain this rather strange scene, one of them being that the boy is standing behind the kettle to hold it steady while the coppersmith drives in the rivets. The stone, ornately decorated in the Rococo style of its day, comes from a house in the Jordaan which, like many other houses, was torn apart for fuel by needy Amsterdammers in the disastrous 'hunger winter' of 1944. As the house formerly abutted on the Koperslagersgang – Coppersmith's

Passage – we can assume that the stone refers to the occupation of the man who lived there at the time. The city housed many coppersmiths, for jugs, kettles and all sorts of other articles made from copper were among the basic utensils. The great quantity of copperwork (or, at least, that portion of it which is genuine) found today in antique shops bears witness to the fact. The coppersmiths belonged to the smiths' guild, whose patron saint was St. Eloy. This was one of the city's oldest guilds and had a varied membership including, for example, cutlers, locksmiths and even armourers. On the Zeedijk the 'Embden messenger' has been travelling now for over three centuries, be it in a petrified form (26). This is an attractive though slightly damaged stone showing an inhabitant of 17th century Amsterdam with a letter in his left hand and in his right (in those days too, nothing was had for nothing) a well-filled purse. The stone is mentioned in documents dating from 1708, but there is no doubt that it was made some decades prior to 1660, the year in which the present building was erected. More inhabitants: 'The Crowned Bread Eater', who may be a baker on his way to the market with a well-filled basket, trying his own bread (24). Whence he derived the

right to adorn his person with a crown is not known. In addition to stones showing bread-eating Amsterdammers, at one time there were also stones showing ham eaters. There was even a Ham-etersgang – Ham Eaters' Passage – near the Singel, and though it was sealed off in 1871 its existence is attested to still by a memorial stone. Elsewhere in the city, an attractive stone showing three hams has been preserved, further evidence of the important place occupied by this commodity in the daily fare of former times being provided by the numerous houses bearing names such as 'The Golden Ham' and 'The White Ham'. A well-preserved stone in the Nieuwebrugsteeg dating from 1618 and showing the bustle of activity in a sugarloaf confectionary (27). The façade of the well-preserved and carefully restored house to which it belongs is particularly appealing because of the warmth of the orange brick.

And the standard hat of the day (28), which would have been visible wherever one turned in the streets of 17th century Amsterdam. The city had a great many hatter's establishments, and evidence of them is also to be found on façades elsewhere among its streets. One example is shown in photograph 216. Close to the house on

25

IN·D·TURE·DRAGER

the Rozengracht where Rembrandt spent the final period of his life is the house with 'The Three Castors', which reminds us that castors, or beaver hats, were among the headgear worn in former days.

In former centuries peat was an important commodity, being used as fuel for a wide variety of purposes. How important it was is indicated by the size of the peat-porters guild, which at the beginning of the 17th century had 360 members who had been appointed by burgomasters and had taken the oath. In addition to these there were the peat-gatherers, the women who, working in the supply ships, collected the loose peat in baskets. In a small street tucked away behind Rembrandt Square and known as 'In het Land van Belofte-steeg' – In the Land of Promise Alley – there was formerly a stone showing a female peat-gatherer. In the same period there were also somewhat over 200 peat-fillers, women who emptied the peat into baskets again after it had been measured in barrels. Over 70 'lifters' were employed in lifting the baskets on to the shoulders of the

26

27

28

porters. Of the various gable stones dedicated to the peat trade, one is still in its original place (25). When the peat-porter Aernoud Jansz. de Koning had the house built in 1689 he decided to have himself portrayed on the gable stone together with one of the chimneys for whose smoke his own efforts were partly responsible.

The peat-porters formed an important guild and were frequently called in for other jobs. As they had to be able to report immediately for fires, storms and 'other difficulties', it was required of them that they live within the city walls.

Despite the abolition of the guilds, the peat-porters continued to be organized until 1859. Peat itself survived for many decades more, and it was not until after the Second World War that its use virtually ceased.

One can also make the acquaintance of the city's inhabitants through the paintings in the corridor of the Historical Museum: warlike figures such as Captain Boom (15) with his company before Zwolle (1623), and Captain A. Cz. Burg discussing fortification, the latter painted in 1625 by W. van Valckert (29).

29

23-29 Inhabitants of Amsterdam: 23 and 24 in the St. Luciënsteeg. 25 on 76 Kerkstraat. 26 on 84 Zeedijk. 27 on 13 Nieuwebrugsteeg. 28 in the St. Luciënsteeg. 29 Painting by W. van Valckert (1625) in the corridor of the Historical Museum showing Captain A. Cz. Burg discussing fortification.

and arches, a lower façade made of wood and the cellar-shop so typical of Amsterdam. Fierce lion's heads decorate the corners of the façade, while on a gable stone (33) another lion looks out of a castle gate. Whereas the two crossed keys on the stone helped to give the house the name 'Leiden Castle', in fact they represent the coat of arms of what is now the Russian city of Riga.

The bottom part of the façade was restored to its original state. So too were the shuttered windows, which show how subtly the old builders played with light. In a climate with so many clouded skies and in an age when artificial light was so expensive, it was in people's interests to let in as much natural light as possible. Later, when costly materials were used for covering chairs and walls, they became more sparing with light: it caused the colours to fade. Early interiors were sober, with little furniture, no wall-coverings and nothing on the floor.

The Herengracht (Gentlemen's Canal) has many bends, but only one bend with a capital B. Those who lived on the Bend of the Herengracht could count themselves among the foremost families of old Amsterdam. With a few exceptions, the huge patrician houses

Wandering along streets and canals

Much has been lost in Amsterdam, but at the same time much has been preserved and restored to its original state. Organizations such as the Stichting Stadsherstel (City Restoration Foundation), Monumentenzorg (Monument Care), the Hendrick de Keyser Society, Diogenes and Aristoteles have achieved a great deal both directly and indirectly by helping to

create a better mentality. A fine example of restoration is the Leeuwenburg House (30), sometimes referred to as 'Leiden Castle', which was raised from a deplorable condition to new splendour in the 1940s. It is once more a beautiful Renaissance house, with everything that that implies: a regular step gable, stone ornamentation, cross windows with shutters

32

in this section of the city are now used as offices (32). The costly interiors have been partly preserved. Despite the traffic, the Bend has retained much of its old dignity.

Another example of restoration, this time just an ordinary house (31). A pleasure to look at; as is the tower of the Zuiderkerk (South Church) (34), seen at its best from the Groenburgwal. A festive tower with a carillon which regularly makes itself heard.

33

30 Leeuwenburg House, 14 Oudezijds Voorburgwal. 31 House on Nieuwe Zijdskolk. 32 Part of the Bend of the Herengracht. 33 Leeuwenburg House gable stone. 34 Zuiderkerk tower seen from the Groenburgwal.

34

35

36

The River Amstel, previously the city's main artery, seen from the Hoge Sluis (Top Lock) (35) with other locks in the foreground, beyond them the wooden Magere Brug (Skinny Bridge), and in the distance the towers of the Oude Kerk and the Zuiderkerk (36). The 's-Gravelandseveer (37) is a part of the Amstel whose name ('veer' means ferry) reminds us of the packet boats that plied the inland waterways linking Amsterdam with almost every other city. As transport by water was cheap these services survived for a long time, and it was not until the advent of modern road transport that they finally disappeared. Another old and picturesque part of the city is the Oudezijds Voorburgwal (40). Predictably in a city so dominated by shipping, the many different kinds of boats that sailed to and from Amsterdam, either by sea or by inland waterway, are portrayed on innumerable gable stones. The two shown here sailed the inland waterways. The larger of the two stones (38) dates from 1754 and has a fairly small boat resembling the typical one-masted fishing boat. A stone showing a fishing boat can be seen on the Binnenkant (39).

38

37

40

39

35 View of the Amstel from the Hoge
Sluis with Magere Brug and Oude
Kerk and Zuiderkerk towers. 36 The
Amstel from the Magere Brug and (37)
the 's-Gravelandseveer. Gable stones
with boats, on 2 Blauwburgwal (38)
and 51 Binnenkant (39). 40 Oudezijds
Achterburgwal with Oude Kerk seen
from the lock.

41

about the smell in the summer. The observant stroller will continually discover new charms in Amsterdam, along wide canals such as the Kloveniersburgwal (43), and in dark, narrow streets such as the St. Nicolaasstraat (44), near the Nieuwendijk, with its crooked buildings so typical of Amsterdam. Though on a smaller scale, the Jordaan still has many survivals from the old city, one example being the entrance to Anslo's Hof (45), a priceless, intimate little almshouse that after several centuries seemed to be nearing its end when, together with surrounding buildings, it was given a new lease of life through the effort of friends of old Amsterdam. Finally, a row of gables on the Singel in the shadow of the Round Lutheran Church (46).

42

41 Oudezijds Kolk looking towards the Oude Kerk, and (42) with windlasses. 43 55 Kloveniersburgwal. 44 St. Nicolaasstraat between Nieuwe Zijds Voorburgwal and Nieuwendijk. 45 50 and 52 Egelantiersstraat. 46 77 Singel.

The almost unspoilt Oude Zijds Kolk (41) preserves the authentic atmosphere of old Amsterdam, a city of water with warehouses on the quayside and vistas of façades and church towers, in this case that of the Oude Kerk. A fine example of how the former inhabitants succeeded in making their city, not merely inhabitable, but inspiring. The wooden windlasses (42) are still used for regulating the sluice that controls the water level in the city as well as refreshing the stagnant water in the canals – the latter an important function, because in the old days there were many complaints

43

44

45

46

47

48

house there and has handsome windows and a gable stone showing the city of 's-Hertogenbosch. It has long housed a café, which was formerly a meeting-place for artists. The large building which used to be in front of it was demolished, the site being now that of the National Monument in memory of those who died in the Second World War.
Both the interior and the exterior of the Huize van Brienen (49) on the Herengracht have been preserved virtually intact. It now accommodates the Hendrick de Keyser Society, which for decades now has dedicated itself to the preservation of the city's architectural heritage.
A cityscape on the Singel (51) opposite the Spui, just a charming row of

In such a damp city tall, narrow houses were preferred. To be well above the dampness was to be 'high and dry'. And naturally it meant that one looked out at the tops of the surrounding houses, as in 47.
The church in the background is the Sint Nicolaaskerk which, with its dome and towers, is one of the dominant features of the view from the waterfront. Scarcely any tourists find their way to the Binnenkant (50), a quiet inlet in the eastern part of the old city where time has stood still and a large proportion of the houses have been preserved in good condition. If you look at them carefully, you will

notice how tall they are, and be able to imagine how many people and what a quantity of goods these buildings were able to hold. The Binnenkant is close to the waterfront. Those living there could see the ships rounding Pampus island on their way to the city and, on the other side of the broad sea arm, the marshes with the 'Volenwijk'. And as the ships approached the harbour the sight that greeted those on board was the façades along the waterfront.
On the Dam, many a passer-by will be struck by the house known as 'the Wild Man' (48) on the corner of the Pijlsteeg. Built in 1632, it is the oldest

gables which, fortunately for us, have survived through the centuries. Awnings, signboards, cellar-shops and even hoisting beams were important features of the streets of old Amsterdam. The extent to which they enlivened the city can be judged from old pictures. The wooden awnings and the cellar-shops were the subject of many a by-law, because they were

47 View in the Dirk van Hasseltsteeg. 48 'The Wild Man' on the Dam. 49 Steps and part of façade of Huize van Brienen, 284 Herengracht. 50 House on the even-number side of the Binnenkant.

over or on municipal land. In 1565 the 'Rooymeesters' (officials responsible for 'rooilijnen', or building lines) went through the city fixing the widths of streets and alleys and numbers of front steps. Other things which received detailed attention were the heights and widths of outside stairs, cellar-shops and 'lowered windows'. The limits placed at first on the height of cellar-shops were five and a half Amsterdam feet at the front and six feet where they were attached to the house wall, the differential being intended to facilitate drainage. They were allowed to project 1.15 metres out from the façade. Though these dimensions were not large, they were sufficient to enable the occupants to store all sorts of utensils, especially

cooking utensils. It was only later that problems arose, when the structures ceased to be used exclusively for household purposes and came to be occupied. The owners of the houses began renting them to craftsmen. Bootmakers in particular were to be found in these cellar-shops, and it was not until after the war that the last of them disappeared from a workshop on the corner of the Keizersgracht and the Prinsenstraat. Later, some cellar-shops and the adjoining cellars became homes for families. Needless to say, this gave rise to pitiful living conditions, which persisted into the 19th century.

At first the city's governors connived at the appearance of all sorts of additional structures, and the citizens

49

50

51

52

made suitable – and more often, unsuitable – use of the fact. A by-law introduced in 1685 attempted to remedy the situation by levying a municipal tax on the building and possession of a cellarshop on municipal land. The revenues it yielded went to the Governors of the Almshouse – now the Palace of Justice on the Prinsengracht – and benefited the orphans, foundlings and paupers for whom they provided. Photo 52 shows a cellar-shop in beautifully preserved surroundings. The house has a blind cellar-shop facing the canal and one with windows and a door facing the alley.

Houses on the Keizersgracht (53). Far from clashing, the different types and colours fuse into a single whole. The grey sandstone of the façade on the left; next to it the orange-coloured bricks of the house where the painter Han van Meegeren used to live; next to that a façade painted black, and then one in brown brick.

51 Façades on the Singel opposite the Spui. 52 77 Herengracht. 53 Houses on the Keizersgracht, from no. 317 (partly visible) to no. 327.

56

58

55

A row of splendid façades belonging to the Cromhout houses (54) on the Herengracht, designed in 1622 by Philip Vingboons for Jacob Cromhout. The Danish writer Andersen stayed at one of them as the guest of a merchant named Brandt. Those whose curiosity extends beyond streets and canals can make a surprising discovery behind gates and walls. One example is the courtyard of what was once the City Orphanage and is now the Historical Museum. Originally a cloister, the complex changed its function after the Alteration in 1578 to become a home for Amsterdam's orphans. The buildings date from different centuries. Photo 55 shows the oldest portion with its freestone pillars; 57, a gallery with lockers in which working orphans could keep their belongings; and 56, the customary pump, which was always beautifully decorated in the old institutions.

59

57

60

The magnificent typically Dutch quadrangle has been completely restored and is open to the public since the celebration of Amsterdam's 700th anniversary in 1975.

If one wants to get to know Amsterdam, travelling by water (58-59) is just as essential as walking along the canals.

Particularly in the winter months, when the trees have lost their leaves, this method of travel reveals the full beauty of the façades.

Remarkably enough, in old Amsterdam bridges of brick and stone were called locks. The Torensluis (Tower Lock) is a wide bridge over the Singel between the Molsteeg and the Leliestraat (60). The reason for its unusual width is that the Jan Roodenpoort Tower used to stand on it, at the old-city end of the bridge. The bridge and its surroundings have been meticulously preserved in a painting by Eekels (72), which also shows us what Amsterdam lost through thoughtlessness when the tower was demolished in the previous century.

Like almost every open space of any size, the Torensluis was formerly the site of a market. Under the bridge were cellars which were used as cells for people under arrest. When the

bridge was restored, the foundations of the tower were found to be intact. Plans have been put forward for rebuilding the tower with the help of the original drawings, which have been preserved.

54 The Cromhout houses, beginning at 370 Herengracht. 55 Courtyard of the former City Orphanage, now the Historical Museum. 56-57 Pump and lockers in the Orphanage. 58 Amsterdam by water: junction of Prinsengracht and Reguliersgracht and (59) Keizersgracht and Reguliersgracht. 60 Torensluis, on the Singel.

61

62

Understandably, with so many miles of canals of all sizes Amsterdam is not only a city of water, it is also a city of bridges. Taking public and private bridges together, it has almost 1300 of them. Though Amsterdam's bridges are still among the many features that make up its charm, they too have suffered the ravages of time. Beautiful curved bridges were replaced by flat, steel ones which, whereas they met the needs of heavier traffic, did nothing to preserve this important aspect of the city. Fortunately, earlier forms are now being turned to in restoration work, which means that drawbridges and, more especially, arch bridges are once more serving as models. Despite the radical changes which have taken place in the city, the words set down by a grandiloquent writer in 1891 in a work on Amsterdam are still partly true: 'And looking down from the high-arched

bridges of the Reguliersgracht, ever
and again one enjoys a spectacle so
peaceful that it has more about it of a
rustic idyll than of a city. The eye,
turned to the bends, beholds a broad,
whitish ribbon of water below like a
strip of slightly crinkled, glistening
silver paper framed on both sides by a
scalloped, light-absorbing, yellow-
green strip of shadow cast by the tree-
tops on the embankment and lighten-
ing at the outer edge through the
reflection of the brightness that falls
against the base of the brick houses'.
For those travelling by water, the
Reguliersgracht is still an oasis,

*61 Wooden drawbridge over the
Nieuwe Herengracht and the Amstel.
62 Bridge over the Groenburgwal. 63
Corner at the Reguliersgracht. 64 View
over the Reguliersgracht in the
direction of the Thorbeckeplein.*

65 19th century ornamentation on the Amstel's Blauwbrug. 66 Number and year on a bridge next to the Montelbaanstoren.
67 Magere Brug over the Amstel.
68-69 Windlasses on the Haarlemmer Lock and the Amstel Locks.

where little has changed in the surroundings save the means of transportation along its banks.

The corner of one of the 'grachten' and the Reguliersgracht and, more especially, the view over the latter with its many bridges all in a line (63-64) give us cause to be thankful to the people – above all, Jan Veth and his followers – who fought for the preservation of the Reguliersgracht in 1901. At that time it was threatened by a mania for filling in canals in the interests of a quantity of traffic that would seem trivial by present-day standards.

The rural atmosphere mentioned earlier applies particularly to the bridge over the Groenburgwal and the Staalstraat (62). Another wooden bridge more reminiscent of a village than of a major city like Amsterdam is the bridge over the Nieuwe Herengracht and Amstel (61), which was restored some years ago to its former beauty.

The Magere Brug (Skinny Bridge) over the Amstel (67): for modern traffic, an old-fashioned bridge, but it is hardly surprising that it has a special place in the hearts of Amsterdammers,

67

68

who would rather close it to traffic
than replace it with a modern bridge.
To live on the Amstel – now very
fashionable – was formerly not so
smart as to live on the Herengracht or
Keizersgracht. The houses on the
Amstel photographed here (69) have
kept much of their charm. In the foreground are the windlasses of the old
Amstel locks, the Amstel too having
been canalized for many centuries.
The Haarlemmersluis (Haarlemmer
Lock) on the Singel by the Brouwersgracht (68) had the important function
of separating the city's canals from
the tidal inlet, the IJ. The quays,
among them Rouen wharf and London
wharf, were named after the cargo
boats that departed from there.
They were not big ships, as they had
to pass through the narrow lock.
A detail from another bridge over the
Amstel, the Blauwbrug (Blue Bridge),
which was modernized in the last
century and given ornamentation that
people are hesitatingly beginning to
appreciate again (65).
Bridges over the Seine in Paris served
as models and the result was rather
pretentious compared with the
Magere Brug.

69

Towers and churches

Amsterdam had many towers.
Fortunately a number of them are still to be seen, rising above the canals and houses. One of the oldest is the Montelbaanstoren (70-71), which was built in the 16th century far beyond the city walls after the Guelders had made an abortive attack on the shipbuilding yards. The lower part of the octagonal base dates from before 1525. A century later, in 1606, the city had a decorative tower built on what was left of the old defence tower, probably using a design by Hendrick de Keyser. The result was the Montelbaanstoren as it is today, a tower built to please the eye and enhance the status of the district.

In 1611 the tower began to sink, but a large number of hastily summoned citizens were able to right it with the help of long cables.

The Jan Roodenpoortstoren on the Singel's Torensluis (72) was also a decorative tower superimposed on an old defence tower. The meticulously executed painting by Eekels, done in 1766, shows us a beautifully designed tower, but it also captures a moment in the everyday life of the city, with boats on the canal, pedestrians on the bridge and by the water, the uniformity in diversity of the houses, lamp-posts of a type that has survived through the centuries and, in the distance, the dome of the Round Lutheran Church. The tower was placed on the demolition list in 1829 and pulled down the same year as being in a state of decay. When, in the 1960s, restoration work on the adjoining Torensluisbrug uncovered the tower's substructure and it was found that all of the working drawings were housed in the city archives, plans were made to have it rebuilt. Unfortunately, they were to prove unsuccessful. The Torensluis is currently one of Amsterdam's widest bridges, measuring 42 metres from one side to the other. A gable stone on a house close to the bridge reminds us that in former times ships moored here that plied a trade with France, reaching as far a Rouen on the Seine.

The Zuiderkerktoren (South Church Tower) or Zandtoren (Sand Tower), perhaps the city's most beautiful tower after that of the Oude Kerk, is shown here (73) rising above the

72

houses of the Kloveniersburgwal.
More difficult to find is the spire next
to it (74); visible only from the
courtyard of the town hall on the
Oudezijds Voorburgwal, it is a
reminder that the building was
originally a monastery dedicated to
St. Cecilia.

In the Middle Ages there was so dense
a concentration of monasteries in this
area that the street that ran alongside
them was called 'Prayer without end'.
The name has survived, as have the
monastery chapels, though they now
have completely different functions.

*70 The Montelbaanstoren and (71)
detail. 72 Painting by Eekels of the
Jan Roodenpoortstoren on the Torensluis, spanning the Singel. 73 Spire of
the Zuiderkerktoren. 74 Spire of the
former St. Cecilia Cloister, now part of
the town hall.*

73   74

Originally dedicated to St. Nicholas, the patron saint of sailors, the Oude Kerk is the city's oldest church. It was consecrated around 1300, prior to Amsterdam's being separated from Ouderkerk and becoming an independent parish. What it lost in unity through the numerous alterations and extensions that were made in the Middle Ages it gained in capriciousness and charm.

A characteristic Dutch city church, expanding with the city and displaying its original role as a place for Catholic services in a myriad of details.

'An airy, playful whim, an openwork witticism,' the Dutch writer Jan Mens said of the Oude Kerk tower. For anyone standing, for example, on the Hoge Sluis and letting his gaze sweep over the stately Amstel it is also an outstanding feature of the skyline – literally and figuratively (35, left). The present spire was designed by the

simple grave (157). Escutcheons and sepulchral monuments preserve the memories of city councillors and naval heroes such as Cornelis Jansz. de Haen (80). A few of the medieval stained-glass windows have been preserved. The Peace of Munster, which finally brought an end to the Eighty Years' War in 1648, was commemorated with a window in 1656 (84). In one of the chapels the city's privileges were kept for many centuries in a sort of fireproof safe. Houses tightly encircle the church. A vestry has a plaque in the wall with 1571 on it (78-79). One of the oldest and most attractive vistas that Amsterdam has to offer is that through the Enge Kerksteeg to the north porch of the Oude Kerk (81).

Anyone who is walking through the

78

75-76 South side of the Oude Kerk. 77 South porch. 78 Plaque on vestry wall. 79 Part of vestry with neighbouring houses.

city architect, Joost Jansz. Bilhamer, and was erected in 1566 after the substructure had been rebuilt and the thickness of its walls increased to 1.20 metres. The new tower rose to a height of 70 metres and reigned supreme until the building of the 15-metre-higher Westertoren. Bilhamer was naturally aided by a number of assistants, and in 1566 these were awarded by the town council the sum of 20 guilders over and above their normal wage in recognition of the services they had rendered in building the tower. To see this imposing tower at its best it should be viewed from the Oude Kerksplein or the St. Annendwarsstraat (16): a stone base with gallery, above this an octagonal wooden structure with clocks, and

rising above that the sixteen pillars, pinnacles and other ornamentation and, finally, the crown surmounted by a weathercock.

Like most old city churches, the Oude Kerk is surrounded by houses and other small buildings belonging to the church administrators, which accentuate the height of the building. Though externally it still has many reminders of its medieval history, the Oude Kerk has been given a sober, Protestant interior. The 38 altars and all the magnificence of a late medieval church have disappeared. There are no statues in the niches any more, for the Calvinists, who took over the church after the Alteration in 1578, abhorred ostentation. However, the rich history of the centuries that followed still resounds there. Many members of Amsterdam's patriciate lie buried in the Oude Kerk under heavy tombstones, and it is here too that Rembrandt's wife Saskia has her

79

80

Warmoesstraat in the direction of the Zeedijk and, about halfway along it, happens to glance to his right is likely to be thrown out of his stride, because there, at the end of a narrow alley which creates a striking effect of depth, is the porch, built c. 1525 and green with age. The porch has all the features of the flamboyant Late Gothic: an elaborately decorated ogee arch, pinnacles ornamented with foliage, a balustrade and niches for statues. For over three hundred years, however, also these niches have been empty. To the left of the porch is a sepulchral chapel which, though it is of only slightly later date, is wholly imbued with the spirit of the Renaissance and closely related in style to the châteaux on the Loire.

Now that years of restoration work have restored them to their former glory, the south side (76) and the south porch (75) are particularly fine. The visitor entering by the south porch passes under the coats of arms of Emperor Maximilian and his son Philip the Handsome (77), from which

skull (82). Another noteworthy feature of the Oude Kerk is the so-called 'Roodeur' (Red Door), through which Amsterdammers passed to register their intention of marrying (83).

One of the streets leading to the Oude Kerksplein is the Enge Kerksteeg. This narrow street has a number of very old houses, one of the most interesting being no. 4 (85). Restored by the Hendrick de Keyser Society, it is built in a simple Amsterdam Renaissance style.

The façade is divided in two by a single slab of stone, above which are a gable stone, 'The Gilded Winnow' (86), and two attractive cartouches with 'Anno' and '1634'. Consoles carved out of wood are still to be seen in the corners above the door.

Another remarkable feature of the church is the so-called Iron Chapel, which is built into a wall well above the reach of flood waters and can be got to only with ladders. The space is sealed off by an iron and a wooden door and for many centuries was used to house the charters which recorded

82

83

one may deduce that these monarchs made a contribution for the enlargement of the church.

There are also a number of surprising sculptures on the jambs, the strangest of them being a monkey holding a

the birth of the city and laid down its rights.

In 1979 the Old Church was reopened in full splendour after a restoration period which had lasted for nearly thirty years. The woodwork had to be

84

86

renovated, and in the process the original colourful paintwork of vaults and beams was brought to light again by stripping off the coats that had been superimposed on it in the course of the centuries. Through the efforts of carpenters, masons, sculptors and workers in stained glass, this 'hybrid' church has once more assumed its former glory.

80 Memorial to Cornelis Jansz. de Haen. 81 North porch in Enge Kerksteeg. 82 Sculpture on south porch. 83 The 'Red Door'. 84 Stained-glass window commemorating the Peace of Munster. 85 4 Enge Kerksteeg with (86) gable stone 'The Gilded Winnow'.

87

The Nieuwe Kerk (New Church) (87, 90) was erected at the end of the 15th century on the other side of the Amstel, the Nieuwe Zijde (New Side), and became the second parish church. The exterior is now sober, with few decorative elements. The interior, on the other hand, is rich by Calvinist standards, having a magnificent chancel screen, a beautifully carved pulpit and an ornately decorated organ. The stained-glass windows, among other things, have greatly benefited from the restoration work that has been undertaken in the church. Admiral Michiel de Ruyter is buried here, as is the poet Joost van den Vondel. A painting by Jan van der Heyden (90), who has given us so many meticulous portraits of Amsterdam, shows the Nieuwe Kerk in the midst of the daily life of the city. That the Nieuwe Kerk is still without a tower can be blamed on a fire in the town hall on the night of July 7, 1652. The church itself had been damaged by the great fire of 1645. In its aftermath, many alterations were made, and the restoration plans included the building of a tower. This had long been the subject of heated debate, one obstacle being an inability to design a

87 East nave of the Nieuwe Kerk, to the right the dome of the Round Lutheran Church on the Singel. 88 Sundial on the south façade. 89 Column and vault decoration. 90 Dam Square with Nieuwe Kerk and part of town hall, by Jan van der Heyden.

tower that would equal or surpass in beauty that of the Oude Kerk. The clamour for a tower had intensified by the mid-17th century, because by that time the Zuiderkerk and the Westerkerk had become prominent features of the city's skyline, whereas all that could be seen of the Nieuwe Kerk above the surrounding rooftops was its nave. A certain Willem Backer pleaded continually for the building of a tower, and it was the supreme moment in his life when, in 1647, his efforts were rewarded and his son laid the first stone, following preparatory work in which an incredible 6,363 piles had been driven into the ground. Jacob van Campen made designs, the models of two of which can still be seen in the Historical Museum. His labours, however, were in vain. One design was rejected, the other not executed. Among the various reasons for this were, first, that Willem Backer's perseverance was undermined by illness and, second, that the city's administrators were faced with the heavy expenditure called for by plans for a new town hall. The tower would perhaps have been completed if the financial means had not been diverted by the need to start immediately on the construction of a new town hall after the fire in the old one.

An additional factor was that the city's rulers were undoubtedly influenced by their fear that the majestic town hall which was then taking shape on the drawing boards would be overshadowed by a tower that would rise far above it.

Old drawings show how high the building reached (14). Part was demolished in 1785, and part preserved as a sign that the Nieuwe Kerk is in fact an unfinished church. Though it failed to acquire a tower, the church later received an honour that no other building, not even the

Oude Kerk, could match. The constitution stipulating that the king shall take his oath and be inaugurated in the city of Amsterdam, the House of Orange chose the Nieuwe Kerk as the site of this ceremony.

Ter Gouw, the well-known 19th century historian, puts forward other reasons for the tower's not having been built. According to Ter Gouw it was 'the old squabble between Moses and Aaron. Each had his supporters both in the burgomasters' office and in the council chamber. The supporters of Aaron, in their eagerness to serve God's house, wanted the building of the town hall to be stopped and all efforts concentrated on the church tower. The followers of Moses were of the opinion that the city stood in greater need of a new town hall than of a high tower, because it would be a disgrace for Amsterdam to continue to make do with the tattered remains of the old one.

89

90

Towers are part of a city skyline, certainly part of a Dutch skyline, rising up from the water and the flat, treeless meadows. From whichever direction one approached a city, these signs of power and heterogeneity were always the first things one saw. With this in view, in the early 17th century the Amsterdammers built their highest tower, the Westertoren (West Tower), 85 metres high with the famous imperial crown on top (96). The crown is not a replica of the one that Maximilian wore – old paintings from that time show the emperor wearing a crown of a more open design – but is fashioned after a later version of the imperial headdress. Only Amsterdam was granted the privilege of bearing the imperial crown in its coat of arms, but it was a privilege the city came very near to losing. The son of Maximilian I, Philip the Handsome, was not at first disposed to confirm the privileges which his father had granted. Indeed, he declared many of them extinct and invalid. The governors of Amsterdam finally decided to visit the archduke in The Hague with the intent of prevailing upon him to restore them. Philip the Handsome displayed little interest in the interview until the envoys broached the possibility of a new gift, whereupon he showed himself more than willing to reciprocate and within two days – to be precise, on 18 July 1497 – confirmed that Amsterdam would retain the right to bear the crown of the Holy Roman Empire in perpetuity.

91 View of the Westerkerk, painting by A.G. van Schoone (1785-1843).
92-93 The Westertoren in winter and summer seen from the Keizersgracht.
94 Memorial to Rembrandt van Rijn.
95 Organ built in 1682.

96

square entrance (98) gives access to a high, airy interior, which has a magnificent organ with panels by De Lairesse (95), and is still the scene of many different ceremonies.

The Westerkerk (West Church) is the largest and most monumental Protestant church in The Netherlands. Built in the early 17th century by Hendrick de Keyser, it has often been celebrated in song and has been frequently painted, for example by A.G. van Schoone (91). Now as in former times, the tower is well visible from the Keizersgracht in winter, but partly hidden by its tall trees in summer (92-93). A memorial to Rembrandt (94) was later erected in the church, though it is not known with certainty where he is buried. Towards the end of

98

his life his fame faded, and the sober merchant city had little respect for those who were not well-off. Other people of note who found a final resting-place in the Westerkerk are the engraver Romijn de Hooghe, the painter Melchior Hondecoeter, the printer Joan Blaeu, the distiller Lucas Bols and Rembrandt's son, Titus. Hendrick de Keyser died a year after the foundation-stone had been laid for the building. His son Pieter carried on his father's work, making one or two changes in the original design, and saw the church completed in 1631. Many paintings, among them one by Jan ten Compe (100), show us how attractive a part of Amsterdam the Regulierspoort (Regulars' Gate) and its surroundings once were. The Munt-

toren (Mint Tower) is a survival from the former gate, which owed its name to a monastery, the Reguliersklooster, situated just outside the city. That part of the gate complex has been preserved is due to the fact that it was thought a pity to demolish it when the city was extended. Unfortunately, a major fire in 1618 destroyed all but the lower portion of one of the towers. Hendrick de Keyser was commissioned to embellish this with a superstructure, the result being described as early as 1620 as a 'handsome and illustrious spire' (99). The names Schapenplein (Sheep Square) and Kalverstraat (Calf Street) recall that in earlier times farmers drove their sheep, cows, oxen and calves to this corner of the city, and it was because

97

96 Spire of the Westertoren. 97 View of the Westertoren from the Driekoningenstraat, in the foreground the Bartolotti House on the Herengracht. 98 Entrance to the Westerkerk on the Prinsengracht. 99 Spire of the Munttoren. 100 Singel with the Munt and the 'English houses', painted by Jan ten Compe in 1751.

The Westertoren dominates the city in the area of the canals and the working-class district known as the Jordaan, but it stands a long way from the IJ and the waterfront. That is surprising, as one would have expected this symbol of the city's power to have been there. Perhaps in those days the quayside was just seen as a workplace, where money was earned, and nothing else. The Westertoren can often be surprisingly striking in a vista, such as that from the Driekoningenstraat (97). The sturdy, of this that Hendrick de Keyser put an ox on the spire's weather vane rather than the customary cock. In 1640, however, a heavy storm caused the ox to end up in the Singel, whereupon less imaginative builders reverted to the cock, which is still to be seen on the tower. The origins of the name Munt (Mint) lie in the hardships occasioned by the French invasion of 1672. The occupation of Utrecht by the French deprived Amsterdam of its source of coins. As a result, the city was given the right of coinage (which it lost two years later) and it was in this tower that the coins were minted. The name Munttoren has been in use ever since, despite an attempt in 1877 to rechristen the square Sophia Square in honour of the first wife of King William III. Next to the tower stood five houses, which had been built by an Englishman and were therefore known as the 'English houses'. By the time the horse-drawn tram was introduced in 1877 these houses had become somewhat dilapidated and, as they were rather in the way, were demolished. Among the noteworthy events of this period was the pulling down of 'Oostmeyer's Wall'. Students who held their meetings in the Munt assisted the development of the horse-drawn tram by destroying the wall after its owner, one Oostmeyer, had refused to allow it to be demolished.

Lutheran immigrants built their first church in 1632, on the Singel near the Spui (108). The well-known domed

99

101

102

church at the beginning of the Singel was their second church, built in 1670 (101). After several decades of being used for a variety of purposes, the latter building underwent a thorough restoration and has now begun a new life as the conference centre of the Sonesta Hotel.

The Noorderkerk (North Church) (102) has a rather out-of-the-way location, being situated on the Noordermarkt. On the other hand, it forms a very attractive spot on the fringe of the Jordaan, especially on market day, which is Monday. Opinions are divided as to the identity of the architect. Some claim to recognize the hand of the omnipresent Hendrick de Keyser. As he died shortly after the first stone had been

laid in 1620, De Keyser could only have been involved in the preparatory work and the initial phase of construction. Others favour Hendrick Jacobsz. Staets, who designed and supervised the extension of Amsterdam in 1612. The distinctive feature of the Noorderkerk is that its plan is a Greek cross: it has four equal arms, with the pulpit placed in the centre of the church. In his 'Beschrijving van de wijdvermaarde koopstad Amsterdam' (Description of the far-famed merchant city of Amsterdam) M. Fokkens calls it the city's best-designed church, on the grounds that it is the best fitted for holding religious services. Because of this, it served as a model for many other Protestant churches, as far distant as Groningen. An inscription

above one of the entrances informs us that: 'This North Church has been founded for the practice of the Christian religion. The first stone laid on the 15th of June in the year 1620, completed in the year 1623, the first sermon given at Easter'. Handsomely made boards displaying the church's seating plan hang beside the rear entrances, which are still in use. The church has a modest little tower, with a clock and 'Anno 1622' on each of its four sides. Old prints show that what is now the Noordermarktplein (North Market Square) was once a cemetery, which began its existence with the building of the church but was closed in 1688. From a late 18th century engraving by Fouquet we learn that the square was already paved by that time and used for holding a market whose wares included signboards. The antecedents of this market go back to 1627, when the city's governors established a Cloth or Rag Market on the site.

The Noorderkerk was closed at a relatively early stage by depopulation, but is now used for Sunday services and other purposes.

On a bend of the picturesque Kromboomsloot, in the midst of houses and warehouses, is what was formerly the Armenian Church. The church was established by the Armenians in 1714, a warehouse having been bought for the purpose, and closed in 1856 when the membership of the community had dropped from several hundred to one. The Armenian community was involved chiefly in the trade in woven cloths and flourished for many years in Amsterdam, which meant that the members of the Armenian Church

104

were in a position to make donations for its embellishment. Even today the passer-by will be struck by the door and steps that the priest had made in 1749 (103). The elegant doorway is crowned by an Agnus Dei (Lamb of God) enclosed, following the current fashion, in a framework of elaborate curves (104). The mid-18th century origin of the steps is similarly betrayed by the beautiful shapes of the ironwork. The text formed by the strange Armenian letters under the lamb is given in Dutch translation in Jan Wagenaar's 'Geschiedenis van Amsterdam'. The first translation (translated in turn into English) says: 'I, Joannes, Priest, Son of Minas, native of the town of Amasia, having served this church, named The Holy Ghost, for fifteen years, have at my own expense rebuilt this front gate; placed a marble Lamb above it; had made the stone steps and three lower and upper lights, in memory of myself and my late Father and Mother in the Armenian year 1198, that is, in the year 1749'.

The second version says: 'Rebuilt again in the year 1198 of the Armenian era, through renewal of the steps and the three upper and lower shutters, at the expense of the servant of this church of the Holy Ghost, Doctor Johannes Minas-Son from Amasia, in the sixteenth year of his office and in memory of his late parents and himself'.

101 The Domed Lutheran Church on the Singel, now part of the Sonesta Hotel complex. 102 The Noorderkerk on the Noordermarkt. 103 The Armenian Church in the Kromboomsloot and, above the door relief with Armenian text (104).

Amsterdam has many more churches. One of them is the Oosterkerk (East Church), which was erected in 1670 outside the city, on the Eastern Islands, where ships were built and the fleet was fitted out. The Republic's reputation as a refuge for the oppressed soon began to attract large numbers of Lutherans from the German states. In 1632 they built a church on the Singel, shown here (108) in a painting made by De Beijer in 1765. Today the

105 Part of the Zuiderkerk tower. 106 Memorial to Johannes Swammerdam in the Walloon Calvinist Church on the Walenplein. 107 View of the Zuiderkerk from what is now the Waterlooplein, painted by Jan de Beijer.

105

106

107

108

church is used by the university as an
auditorium. In 1758 Jan de Beijer
painted the tower of the Zuiderkerk
from the site that was later drained to
become the Waterlooplein (Waterloo
Square) (107): a typical Amsterdam
scene, with water, a bridge, trees,
people working and, rising above it
all, the graceful arabesque of the
church tower. The Zuidertoren (34 and
105) is one of the finest towers that
Hendrick de Keyser built in Amsterdam. It was a period of rapidly growing prosperity and optimism, and this
is reflected in the tower's combination
of vitality and gracefulness. Among
the features on the Walloon Calvinist
Church on the Walenplein are a
splendid organ and a memorial to
Swammerdam (106), who attended
services there.
Despite the prevailing tolerance, the
city's rulers had difficult decisions to
make as regard two groups, the Jews
and the Roman Catholics. Part of the

108 The Lutheran Church on the
Singel, painted by de Beijer in 1765.
111 Part of the façade of the classicistic
Moses and Aaron Church on the
Waterlooplein, with stones (109-110).

111

112

population had remained faithful to the old religion after the Reformation. The building of Roman Catholic churches was hesitantly connived at, but they must not be recognizable as churches. The result was the appearance of clandestine churches such as Ons' Lieve Heer op solder (Our Lord in the Attic) on the Oudezijds Voorburgwal and the Begijnhof chapel (115). It was not until the 19th century that the Roman Catholics were able to build churches with complete freedom. Built in the classical style of that period, the Moses and Aaron Church (111) on the Waterlooplein still displays stones of the original clandestine church (109-110).

Jews came to Amsterdam from the South and the East. They remained divided in religious practices and were soon allowed to build their own synagogues. The city has never had a ghetto, but a district did develop in

113

114

which Jews were in the majority. The Portuguese synagogue (112), built in 1671, is a dignified and substantial edifice surrounded by smaller buildings and bears witness to the prosperity and self-respect of a community with rich cultural traditions. On the opposite side of the J.D. Meijerplein is the Dutch-Israelite synagogue (113-114), a block of buildings that comprises several rooms for service and reached its present form after more than a century of expansion.

115

112 Gable stone with Hebrew and Dutch text, Portuguese synagogue (1671) on the J.D. Meijerplein. 113 Part of the façade and (114) detail of the entrance of the Dutch-Israelite synagogue on the same square. 115 Entrance of the Begijnhof chapel.

The glory of the façades

Early Amsterdam was not only built on wooden piles: all of the houses were of wood. A number of devastating fires were needed, such as that in 1452, before a by-law was passed requiring that new houses be built of brick or stone. It was not until 1521, however, that Emperor Charles V allowed the town council to compel 'the rich and powerful citizens and inhabitants' to knock down their wooden houses and replace them with dwellings made of brick.

Naturally, some time was needed for this measure to be put into effect. Every year a number of wooden houses were demolished and replaced by brick houses, the city contributing to the costs where owners were unable

116

117

Amsterdam's oldest houses: on the Zeedijk (116) and in the Begijnhof (117). They are the only wooden houses of the city which have been preserved.

to meet them. If you walk from the Prins Hendrikkade in the direction of the Zeedijk you will pass one of the two surviving part-wooden houses (116). The façade dates from the second half of the 15th century, at which time the side walls were already of brick. The adjoining house, no. 3, formerly known as 'Daniel in the Lions' Den', still broadly corresponds to the illustration on the famous map produced by Cornelis Anthoniszoon in 1514. The second wooden house is in the Begijnhof (117), to whose inhabitants it became an even greater source of pride when restoration work undertaken in the 1950s showed it to be the older of the two.

Traffic following the route to Haarlem from the Damrak passes the Spaanse Huis (Spanish House) (122), situated on the corner of the Singel and the Droogbak. The house probably dates from the early years of the 17th century, the evidence for this being extant deeds of sale according to which one Jan Willemszoon, by trade a vendor of chamois leather, bought part of the land for 1,400 Carolus guilders. In 1603 he resold it to Claes Rodenburgh, who presumably had the house built. The façade has a gable with eleven steps and a gable stone showing a wheelbarrow (120). The latter may have been the work of the man who owned it around the middle of the 17th century, whose name,

according to the ground-tax register for 1658, was Hendrick Jansz. Cruy-wagen (Wheelbarrow). On the other hand, the possibility can not be excluded that it was the gable stone on the house he had bought that caused him to adopt the name 'Wheelbarrow'. The building was used for many years as a ferry-house, which may be part of the reason that it acquired a coffee-house at a very early date.
It is not known with certainty why the building came to be called the 'Spanish House'. As it was erected so many years after the Spanish period the explanation can not be sought in Spanish builders or owners. The most plausible theory is that Spaniards lived in it, carving Spanish words in

the beams of the attic. The site lay outside the walls in the Spanish period, and was not absorbed by the city until the first extension was undertaken in 1585.
Aside from impressive patrician houses the Keizersgracht has some step-gabled warehouses (121), the 'Greenland warehouses', which are among the most interesting that Amsterdam has to offer. Lacking the sturdy, massive quality of the ware-houses on the Brouwersgracht and the Realengracht, they were built in the early 17th century and provided with three step gables, a type rarely found on warehouses.
The Northern Company, which pro-bably had them built, installed special

119

120

118

122

121

123

124

tanks for storing the whale oil that the whalers brought back from the waters around Greenland and elsewhere. Of the hundred tanks used by the company in its heyday, one has been preserved in its original condition. The warehouses on the Keizersgracht also bear witness to the fact that, in the early days of the city's expansion, merchants and other businessman lived close to their work. The goods they dealt in were stored in the attic of their own house.

It was only later, when prosperity reached unprecedented levels, that house and warehouse were separated. The houses are appartments now. The passion for decoration is a typical characteristic of the Dutch. If you live beneath grey skies, you have to use your imagination to give your life some colour. In the early 17th century, builders often made use of small bricks that were almost orange in colour, and enlivened their façades with small blocks of stone, in many cases decorated with human heads (119), lion's heads (142) or masks (131). An average example of such a house is to be seen on the Geldersekade (118) – not

strikingly ornamented, not the work of a great master, but nonetheless gay and colourful.

Other examples of the beautiful ornamentation so abundant in Amsterdam are to be seen on a house on Oudezijds Voorburgwal (123), with a façade belonging to the school of Hendrick de Keyser; on the Makelaers Comptoir on Nieuwezijds Voorburgwal (124), and many other buildings. One of the most attractive houses in Amsterdam is the 'House on the Three Canals' (129), with the Oudezijds Voorburgwal running along the front, the Grimburgwal along one side and

118 97 Geldersekade. 119 Sculpted head on 2 Prinsengracht. 120 Gable stone 'The Wheelbarrow' on the Spanish House, 2 Singel. 121 The Greenland Warehouses, 38-44 Keizersgracht. 122 The Spanish House, 2 Singel. 123 Part of the façade of 20 Oudezijds Voorburgwal. 124 Stone giving year, Makelaers Comptoir, 75 Nieuwezijds Voorburgwal.

126

the Oudezijds Achterburgwal along the back. For the last of these streets one should actually write 'O.Z. Agterburgwal', because this splendid building does not display the name of the street on a common-or-garden enamel sign, but on a block of sandstone, using the old spelling. The designation 'Oudezijds Voorburgwal' is also incorrect, for anyone trying to find his way will discover an equally fine stone telling him that the street is called the 'Fluweelenburgwal' – a name which takes us back in history to the time when there were green meadows beyond the circle of the canals and when the wealthy citizens of Amsterdam, wearers of 'fluweel' (velvet), lived in stately homes on the canal that is now the Oudezijds Voorburgwal. According to Ter Gouw, who made such a thorough study of street names in the second half of the 19th century, those who lived here were the rich, who 'dress in caffa, silk and velvet'.

The house was built in 1609 by Claes Adriaensz. in the simple Haarlem Renaissance style with, among other things, the same semicircular arches above the windows as are seen on the 'Lompert' house in the Nieuwe Brugsteeg.

Painstakingly restored in 1909, the

128

building has been the home of many well-known Amsterdammers, including Real and Roeters.

Its occupants had a beautiful view (but then, who did not in those days?) of the Grimburgwal and of the Oudemanhuis Gate and the gate of the Binnengasthuis, both of which are still there. A third gate, which gave access to the Heerenlogement on the opposite side of the Grimburgwal, was moved to 367 Keizersgracht in 1876. How many millions have stood face to face with Frans Banning Cocq and his companions of the Night Watch? However many it may be, another inhabitant of the city in its heyday is undergoing a somewhat similar fate as a result of his having been portrayed in a painting displayed in the corridor of the Historical Museum, which left the Kalverstraat with the Gedempte

127

Begijnesteeg. The man in question is Lieutenant Willem Backer, who forms part of a group which includes his captain and burgomaster Abraham Boom Pietersz. (15). At 28 years of age, Willem Backer was in his prime and served in the company that was sent to defend Zwolle in 1623. He crops up a number of times in Amsterdam's history. When the painting was executed he was in the first year of his marriage to Brigitta Spiegel, the daughter of Laurens Jansz. Spiegel, Lord of Achttienhoven and chief landholder of the Beemster, as well as being a soap-maker on what is now the Kattegat but was formerly the Nieuwe Zijds Melkmarkt.

The two houses that Spiegel ('Mirror') had built (125-126) still rest against the broad flank of the Round Lutheran Church, are still called the 'Gouden en de Silveren Spiegel' ('The Gold and the Silver Mirror') and still have mirrors pointing in four directions on top of their gables, in honour of their name. Willem Backer later inherited the houses, and the burgomaster's room is still preserved in the restaurant that now occupies the building. This same Willem Backer was – as burgomaster and leader of the Calvinists in the council – the chief advocate for the completion of the Nieuwe Kerk tower. It was a great day indeed for him when, on July 20, 1647, his son Cornelis laid the first stone of the tower. However, plans for building a new town hall were in an advanced stage and this was later to give rise to problems, in that some members of the council were of the opinion that two such costly projects could not be undertaken simultaneously. The issue was finally settled by the fire in the old town hall. Willem Backer's protracted struggle for a tower had been in vain. It is not known whether the two things are connected, but three months after the decision had been taken not to finish the tower, Backer died, at 57 years of age. Something of these events has been preserved for posterity in a funeral poem by Six van Chandelier.

When you stand in front of these houses, you can not help realizing that almost all the streets here were formerly canals and that the buildings used to be much closer together. The twins are worth studying. In the details you can see how much care was taken with the construction of an ordinary house: variety in colour and form, ornamentation, cramp irons and the whole façade resting on a lower front of wood.

125 'The Gold and the Silver Mirror' on the Hekelveld with detail of the façade (126). 127 Stone on the 'House on the Three Canals' giving the former name of Oudezijds Voorburgwal. 128 House on the 81 Herengracht, originally built in 1590. 129 Part of the façade of the 'House on the Three Canals'.

129

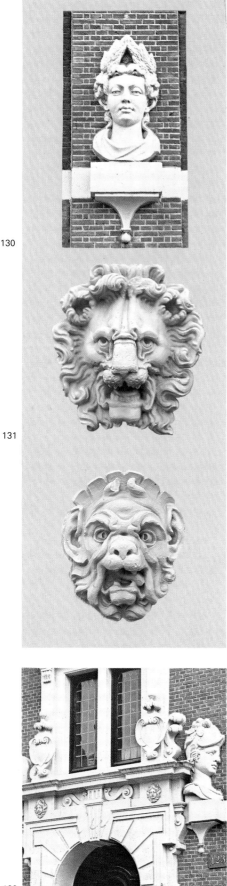

130

131

132

133

One of the most beautiful houses on the Keizersgracht, if not in the whole of Amsterdam, is the 'Huis met de Hoofden' (House with Heads) (134). It is striking in several respects, among them a façade that breathes the spirit of Hendrick de Keyser, its attractive orange colour and – above all, perhaps – the larger than life-size heads projecting from the wall (130, 132, 133). These are assumed to represent Greek and Roman gods and goddesses and have been identified as Apollo, Ceres, Mars, Minerva, Bacchus and Diana on the evidence of their headdress.

It is possible that there was formerly a seventh figure commemorating the victim of a murder that is said to have taken place in the house, and that this murder provides the explanation for the other heads. There is also a popular version, known as the tale of 'The maid and the six robbers', according to which the heads are those of burglars who were decapitated one by one by a sturdy maid-servant. That the façade is so strikingly attractive is also due to the abundance of smaller decorative sculptures, including garlands, clusters of assorted fruits and the traditional lion's heads and masks displaying a wide variety of expressions (131). The house was begun in 1622. It was probably designed by Pieter de Keyser for a French merchant called Schier, but was shortly afterwards sold to Lodewijk de Geer, a prominent merchant and arms manufacturer. Lodewijk's descendants continued to inhabit this Renaissance patrician house until 1746, when it was sold to a Zealander. It has changed hands many times since then and is now an office building. A gable stone above the doorway and a memorial plaque of the Winkler Prins Foundation announce that the Czech educational reformer Comenius stayed in the house. Comenius died in Naarden, a fortress city east of Amsterdam, where his mausoleum is still visited by hundreds of Czechs every year, as well as by people of other nationalities.

134 The 'House with Heads', 123 Keizersgracht, with details (130-133) of its rich ornamentation.

Two neighbouring houses on the Herengracht that differ widely in style and yet go extraordinarily well together: the Bartolotti House and the Messina House. The former (135) was built by Willem van den Heuvel, a banker who adopted the name Bartolotti. A simpler version of the same style is seen in the house known as 'The Wild Man' on the Dam (48). The second of the two neighbours is remarkable for its exterior, for its interior and also for its present function. What makes it so notable externally is the width of its façade and the use of sandstone, a costly and therefore little used material at the time when Michiel Pauw (1590-1640) commissioned Philip Vingboons to design it. This was Vingboons' first commission in Amsterdam. The original house dates from 1618, but it was rebuilt in 1638 for Pauw, whose coat of arms flanked by two handsomely coiffured winged lions was placed on the sturdy, low gable.

The lions are almost certainly explained by his being a knight of the Venetian order of St. Mark. The façade is well preserved on the whole, though at some stage – doubtless during the French occupation – Pauw's coat of arms was erased. The house's interior is one of the most beautiful in Amsterdam. Since the Museum of Dramatic Art ended its peregrinations here fifteen years ago, it is also readily accessible. In this building the visitor can get some idea of the almost un-Dutch luxury of Amsterdam's patrician houses. The passages have an abundance of stuccowork done by Jan van Logteren Ignatiuszoon in the mid-18th century, while the rooms display painted hangings by Jacob de Witt and canvases by Isaac de Moucheron. In Amsterdam's early days many monasteries were to be found in the district lying between the Rokin and the Kloveniersburgwal. Numerous traces of them have survived in later buildings and in foundations. The history of the Prinsenhof, for example, goes back to the Alteration in the year 1578 when many monasteries were closed and confiscated. The city's governors designated the St. Cecilia Cloister as a reception centre for important persons. The name Prinsenhof (Princes' Court) is adequately explained by a list of Dutch notables that includes William the Silent,

the princes Maurice of Nassau and Frederick Henry, and William II, and a list of foreign guests that includes the Earl of Leicester, the French queen Marie de Médicis and an English queen. When the Oude Zijds Heerenlogement took over this function, the entire building was placed at the disposal of the Admiralty and officially became known as Admiralty Court. The name, however, did not catch on. The abolition of the Admiralty in the Batavian Republic led to the building's being converted into a customhouse. It acquired its present function in 1808, when Louis Bonaparte took over the town hall on the Dam for himself and the royal household. The town council was obliged to move to the Prinsenhof, where it has remained ever since. There can be few buildings in the old city that are known to as many people as the Prinsenhof. Aside from being the town hall, it is the office for the registration of births, marriages and deaths, and therefore the place where the civil marriage ceremony is performed. Anyone waiting in front of the town hall is advised to look up at the splendid pediment that adorns the

135

136

137

Prinsenhof (137).

The present structure dates from the 1660s. The relief on the pediment is by Jan Gijseling and shows the Dutch Lion, in the middle, guarding the Dutch 'Garden'. The lion is holding the Admiralty's coat of arms with two anchors, while the two cherubs above him are crowning him with a garland. Flanking him are Neptune with his trident, other deities of the sea, dolphins and a variety of objects that would be needed in fitting out a 17th century ship. The visitor to the Prinsenhof should also have a look at the elegant pump in the middle of the courtyard, which has stood in the same spot for centuries, its taps emerging from awful mouths.

138

139

135 Bartolotti House, 170-172 Herengracht. 136 Bartolotti House with the Messina House, now the Museum of Dramatic Art, 168 Herengracht. 137 Tympanum of the Prinsenhof, now the town hall. 139 Pump in the courtyard and (138) detail of one of the taps.

140

141

142

The gables on pages 68-69 are usually called bell gables because of their resemblance to the cross-section of a bell. The bell gable is Amsterdam's most characteristic gable. Hundreds of them are still to be seen, but there used to be many more. In the late 18th century especially, it was common practice to replace a bell gable with a flat frame gable.

According to the fasion of the day, the latter was more distinguished. Examples of the simplest type of bell gable are to be seen on the Prinsengracht (140) and on the corner of the Geldersekade and the Nieuwe Jonkerstraat (142). They are made almost entirely of brick: stone had to come from abroad and was therefore expensive. A more elaborate version is found on the Oudezijds Voorburgwal with the name of the house at the top, 'De Vijgenboom' (The Fig Tree) (141). Once the bell gable had established itself in Amsterdam, builders began to enjoy experimenting with it.

People who had a house built did not want a standardized product. Everyone gave his individual touch to his own house and the designers of bell gables had sufficient imagination to think of a new variation every time. Though somewhat slower than today, taste and fashion were constantly changing. When the decorative elements of the Baroque and the Rococo

reached the Low Countries from Italy and, especially, France they were eagerly taken up by the gable designers. If you stroll along the canals and streets of the old city you will see samples of all bygone fashions.

A few examples. A 'French' bell gable with Rococo ornamentation on a house in the Jordaan (143). Another on a second house in the same district, this time with a castle at the top (144). The gable with the 'Sieperse Kat' ('Cyprian cat', or tabby) (145) under the apex, telling us something about pets in that age, or perhaps about the island with which the owner traded. Designing and constructing such a gable was a job for a craftsman and was carried out with great care. The back of the gable was usually anchored as a protection against storms. As stone weathers very quickly in the damp Amsterdam climate it was painted, and repainted.

Alongside the bell gable a new type developed, known as the neck gable. Again, connoisseurs distinguish between a wide variety of sub-types and related designs. Neck gables are usually tall, slender structures with pilasters, 'oeils-de-boeuf', side-pieces and a wealth of other decorative features. The originator of the neck gable was Philips Davidsz. Vingboons or Vinckeboons (1607-1678), whose influence on Amsterdam's architecture was so great that – aside from 'Vingboons gable' as an alternative for neck gable – the term Vingboons style is used to describe the narrow houses of governors and merchants that are still everywhere to be seen along Amsterdam's canals. His work is known from those of his houses that have survived, but also from a book with 61 plates depicting his principal buildings. Vingboons' father, who came to Amsterdam from Mechelen, had three artistic sons, of whom Philip was undoubtedly the most gifted. His brother Justus was also an architect and is known, among other things, for the Trippenhuis on the Kloveniersburgwal, a double house with a single, broad façade that differs radically indeed from the 'Vingboons style'.

140 Plain bell gable on 40 Prinsengracht. 141 More ornate bell gable on 42 Oudezijds Voorburgwal. 142 Detail of 97 Geldersekade, corner of Geldersekade and Nieuwe Jonkerstraat with left bell gable 143 Bell gables on 60 Leliegracht, Eerste Boomdwarsstraat (144) and 36 Leliegracht (145).

143

144

145

146

and the façade was restored to its original state, among other things by replacing missing Corinthian capitals and installing new windows.

A cartouche under the hoisting beam gives the date, 1656, in a rather more difficult form than usual by employing Roman numerals.

Side-pieces are a characteristic feature of Amsterdam's neck gables. They fill the right angle formed by the eaves and the neck and are decorated with a variety of creatures aside from dolphins, including lions, tritons and gods and goddesses from Classical mythology. Neptune on a dolphin (148), on the Herengracht, is a good example of what could be done when designers gave their imaginations free rein.

The Kalfsvelsteeg (Calfskin Alley), which comes out on the Rokin, is one of a great number of small streets and alleyways whose names have a history. When Susanna van Gansepoel bought a plot of land here in 1661 the deed of sale described it as being on 'the east side of the Rocking, on the corner of Calf's Skin Alley, where the Calf's Skin hangs'. One theory is that there was a calfskin workshop in the

147

There can be no doubt that the seafarers who sailed in such numbers the endless seas between Amsterdam and the East Indies were fascinated by the dolphins they saw leaping and plunging among the waves. The numerous dolphins decorating Amsterdam's merchant houses bear witness still to the tall stories they must have brought home about these graceful animals. The favourite sites for these stone memorials of romantic seafaring yarns are the sides of neck gables. The biggest specimens are to be found on a building on the Oudezijds Voorbugwal (146) with their heads resting on the eaves and their bodies and tails against the pillars that enclose the neck gable. Garlands of shells entwine the dolphins, who have survived the almost 325 years of their existence with little sign of wear. When the house was restored some years ago the dolphins were cleaned

148

146 Ornate neck gable with side-pieces depicting dolphins, 18 Oudezijds Voorburgwal. 147 Part of the gable of 91 Rokin. 148 Neck gable with dolphins and sea gods, 504 Herengracht.

alley producing drums for the civic guards and other military units. Another is that a craftsman or dealer in calfskin lived here whose trade was in the gold leather that was so popular as a wall-covering among wealthy Amsterdammers. In those days the Rokin was a narrow waterway. The house built on the plot mentioned in the deed was completed in 1664 and is still one of the ornaments of what has now become a busy thoroughfare for road traffic. It was long known as the 'House of the Griffins' (147), because this was what the sidepieces against the gable were taken to represent. In fact, they are eagles, with their sharp-beaked heads pointing in both directions along the Rokin. The house was built in the Vingboons style using Bentheim sandstone. In addition to the eagles holding coats of arms, it is decorated with garlands, festoons and elaborate oeils-de-boeuf. The choice of eagles doubtless arose from the name Adelaer (Eagle). Coert Siwertsen Adelaer married Anne Pelt, the daughter of the woman who had built the house, Susanna van Gansepoel, and would have lived there with her if his appointment as admiral of the Danish fleet had not obliged him to move to Denmark. An important man in his day, Coert Adelaer served under Maarten Harpertsz. Tromp and fought with the Venetians against the Turks, as a result of which he was entered in the marriage register as 'Chevalier of St. Mark and the Great Senate of Venice'. During the restoration undertaken in the early 1960s, missing ornamentation was replaced and the two coats of arms held by the eagles were given their original colours.

The very elaborate coat of arms of Coert Adelaer is on the left; on the right (147) is a simpler design showing a silver and red cross ancrée on a blue shield. One of the quarters of Adelaer's coat of arms shows a left arm coming out of a cloud, the hand holding a sword on which the head of a Turk is depicted. This is said to refer to one of his many martial exploits, the story being that, though himself wounded, he cut off the head of the Turk Ibrahim Pasha with his left hand.

149

An extraordinarily well-preserved section of canal façade is to be found on the Herengracht at its junction with the Leidsegracht. A stroller on the opposite side of the canal can get a fine view of it from the Beulingstraat. On closer inspection he will undoubtedly be struck by two neck gables with life-size figures as side-pieces (149). One senses immediately that these are houses with a history. Both houses were completed in 1665. The first occupant of no. 390 was a silk merchant called Jan Eyghels, and he probably had the gable figures executed after consulting the person building the other house.

Each gable is flanked by a man and a woman holding the two ends of a cord symbolizing their marriage bond. The cord disappeared at some stage from the house on the left, no. 392, and it was not replaced when the building was restored. In the troubled times of

the Patriotic movement the house on the right was occupied by Captain De Wilde of the civic guards, who opposed the Prussians when they penetrated to Ouderkerk in 1787. Each of the figures is holding an escutcheon with one hand, but there are no coats of arms on them. It is possible that, as with so many other houses, the coats of arms were removed during the French occupation. As the new rulers were not too kindly disposed at first to the nobility of the Stadholders period, it was generally advisable not to annoy them with displays of this kind. The houses are of sandstone and have ribbons of flowers alongside the windows. They are thought to have been built by Justus Vingboons, one of the architects of the rich Baroque period and a brother of Philip Vingboons, whose houses are to be seen throughout the city.

Many a visitor to the town hall on the

149 Neck gables with ornate sculptures, 394 Herengracht. 150 Gable with heads of oxen on the Oudezijds Voorburgwal opposite the town hall. 151 Gable of the 'House with the Noses', 232 Oudezijds Voorburgwal. 152 Mercury, the God of Trade, on 326 Singel. 153 Two cornucopias on 258 Singel.

Oudezijds Voorburgwal will have been struck by the oxen heads on a gable belonging to a building on the opposite side of the canal (150).
Neither the present nor the previous function of the building explains them. At one time, however, it housed the Meat Market. The market was first housed in a chapel of the St. Peter's Cloister, and later extended by the addition of a chapel from a neighbouring monastery. When the old buildings were pulled down in 1779, a new market was built and given

appropriate ornaments on its gable. At that time there were almost 50 butcher's stalls in the building; it also housed various guilds and had a dissecting room for surgeons.

Three oddities are to be found on the façade of a house on the Oudezijds Voorburgwal: a strange figure on top of the gable, an equally strange coat of arms and a gable stone with the word PARIJS (151). Though this last is the Dutch name for the French capital, in fact it has nothing to do with it. The house was bought in 1626 by one Pieter Parijs, who had his name put on the façade.

The stone was kept when, in 1715, a new house was built on the site by a wealthy money changer – Jan Frederik Mamuchet, Lord of Houdringen – who decorated its neck gable with his coat of arms. The design on the coat of arms is explained by the fact that the name Mamuchet can be translated as beak. It is not known whether the family had a hereditary disposition to hawk noses and whether it is for this reason that the people on the coat of arms are portrayed as having them. At any rate, the building came to be known as the 'House with the Noses'.

Opinions differ as to the identity of the figure on top of the gable, some people having claimed that it was a Saracen, others a mythological figure, yet others a faun, and various other people, various other things.

A house on the Singel (153) testifies to Amsterdam's status as a merchant city by using Mercury, the God of Trade, for one of the side-pieces. The gable of another house on the same canal (152) adds a festive note to its stern dignity by means of two cornucopias.

150

151

152

153

154 Part of the façade of Rembrandt's house in the Jodenbreestraat (no. 4). 155 140-142 Singel, home of Frans Banningh Cocq. 156 Gable stone on 184 Rozengracht. 157 Tombstone of Saskia in the Oude Kerk. 158 Part of the gable of the Saaihal in the Staalstraat. 159 Rembrandt's 'Staalmeesters' (Rijksmuseum). 160 Burgomaster Jan Six (218 Amstel).

154

155

exterior is that the edges of the gable are carved in the form of draped cloth, the cloth continuing on to the wall below the vases decorating the corners of the gable (158). It was in this building that Rembrandt painted the 'Staalmeesters', sampling officials of the Drapers' Guild who sought him out in the sombre years when he was living on the Rozengracht. The painting (159) shows the group of officials whose job it was to certify the quality of cloth after subjecting it to a number of tests. After hanging in the building until 1771, the painting was transferred to the town hall on the Dam and later to the Rijksmuseum.

The gable also displays a date and a beautiful coat of arms of Amsterdam, and is completed by an imperial crown surmounting its horizontal upper edge. The present building is a survival from a large complex that had its main entrance on the Groenburgwal. Among other things, the building later served as a police station and a chemical laboratory. The Nobel Prize winner Van 't Hoff worked there before moving to Berlin. Restoration after the First World War saved the

157

Running alongside the Amstel between Kloveniersburgwal and Groenburgwal is the Staalstraat, a short, narrow street with a very special building. The word 'staal' means steel, but it also means sample. The reference in this case is to the samples of cloth inspected by the sampling officials in the Saaihal (Serge Hall), a building designed by Pieter de Keyser (a son of Hendrick) and erected in 1641. One notable feature of the

158

159

building from decay.

A well-preserved building in what is now the Jodenbreestraat was for many years the home of Rembrandt (154). His last house was on the Rozengracht (156). Rembrandt died in 1669 and was buried in the Westerkerk. His first wife, Saskia van Uylenburgh, is buried in the Oude Kerk, where a simple stone (157) marks the probable site of her grave. Another famous painting by Rembrandt – the portrait of burgomaster Jan Six (160) – has not been transferred to the Rijksmuseum but hangs in a house on the Amstel where, eight generations later, Six's descendants still live. Also associated with Rembrandt is the house on the Singel (155) that was the home of Frans Banningh Cocq, one of the main figures in the 'Night Watch'.

The house was also the house of Hendrik Laurensz. Spieghel (1549-1612), well known Dutch author and compiler of the first modern Dutch grammar.

160

Warehouses make a very distinctive contribution to the visage of Amsterdam. The Arsenal (161) on the Waterlooplein is one of many impressive warehouse complexes.

Built in 1610 on what was then the Leprozengracht (Leper Canal) for the storage of grain and peat, it was under the supervision of the Oude Zijds Huiszittenmeesters, who had their offices in the Nes. Huiszittenmeesters were the officials responsible for administering poor relief to needy persons living at home. Their responsibilities were limited to a given district, so that in addition to the Oude Zijds (Old Side) there were also the Nieuwe Zijds (New Side) Huiszittenmeesters. The extent of poor relief can be gauged to some extent by looking at the size of these warehouses, which are seen here in

shown on the seal of the city.
The hundreds of old warehouses still
existing in Amsterdam are so solidly
built that they will survive for centuries to come. The oldest date to
be found in the city is that on the
Waag, in the Nieuwmarkt, where an
inscription carved in stone informs us
that the Sint Anthoniespoort was
begun in 1488. The second oldest,
1550, is on the façade on a warehouse
on the Oudezijds Voorburgwal – specifically, on the low arch of a cellar
entrance (168), where Joost van den
Vondel may have passed daily when
he was employed by the adjoining
Lending Bank. There are many warehouses along the Brouwersgracht, one
group being formed by 'Het Groene
Hert' (The Green Deer) (166), 'De Ezel'
(The Donkey) and adjoining buildings

*161 The Arsenal, warehouse on the
Waterlooplein. 162 'De Ezel' and other
warehouses on the Brouwersgracht.
163 Hoisting beam on warehouse on
the Kromboomssloot. 164 Hoisting
beam with windlass on the Prins
Hendrikkade.
165 Covered hoisting beam on warehouse on the Brouwersgracht. 166 'Het
Groene Hert' warehouse on the
Brouwersgracht.
167 Gable of warehouse on the West
India Company on the corner of the
Prins Hendrikkade and 's Gravehekje.
168 Arch with date, 300 Oudezijds
Voorburgwal.*

their refreshed state after being recent-
ly restored. They were used chiefly
for grain and peat, but also for such
things as butter and even coffins.
Food and fuel were distributed to
those who found themselves in difficulties either through seasonal circumstances (especially in the winter
months when there was no shipping)
or for other reasons.
One of the Huiszittenmeesters' charges
under the latter heading was the care
of foundlings. On the corner of the
Waterlooplein and the Mr. Visserplein
their office is still to be seen with its
attractive courtyard and, on the back
wall, a stone depicting the cockboat

(162), some of which have been converted into houses – young people especially find it romantic to live by a canal with massive beams above their heads. Although all of Amsterdam's warehouses were built for the same purpose, storage, they were often given distinctive exteriors, including a variety of attractive gables, some of them not very different from those of ordinary houses. The hoisting beams, which were operated from inside with a windlass, had to be strong enough to lift heavy loads. One example of a beautiful gable complete with covered

170

171

172

169

hoisting beam is that on the building of the West India Company (167), which hoped to make as large a fortune as the East India Company.
Many hoisting beams have survived, but not many covered ones. The latter, with their roofed structures to afford protection against the elements, set certain warehouses apart, such as those on the Kromboomssloot (163), the Prins Hendrikkade (164-165).
A merchant city on the water's edge, tall narrow houses with large attics, ships in the port with all sorts of merchandise in their holds, transport everywhere, especially by water, and everywhere people busily engaged in moving goods from one place to another. Is it surprising, then, that

Amsterdam is the city of hoisting beams? This means of vertical transport, born of trade, became and has remained one of the normal attributes of any house. A rich variety of styles was achieved: for example by adding a woman's head, as on the Singel (172), or two heads in the Rococo manner, as on the Leidsegracht (171). A house in the Westerstraat has a simple hoisting beam, but above it is a lion with a golden crown (170). The hoisting beam was an integral part of the façade, not an addition to it. It was taken into account in designing the house, and if the builder had an inspiration or the owner requested it, was given the same careful attention as the door or the gable.

173

175

Anyone with an eye for detail will be struck by the variety and beauty of the windows over the front doors of so many of Amsterdam's houses. Their purpose is to allow light to enter the passage behind the door, and they came into fashion in the 18th century when houses acquired a long passage with the various rooms leading off it.

The practice soon developed of furnishing these windows with an iron frame as a protection against breakage, burglary, etc., which meant that the smiths were given numerous opportunities to indulge their imaginations and artistic instincts. A house on the Nieuwezijds Voorburgwal is one of many examples of how eagerly they

made use of them: the window bears the flamboyantly wrought initials of Anthonie Warin, who had the house built around 1740 (176).
A house on the Rusland (174) has a window that is dated 1767 and displays all the features of classicism. A few doors along, an exceptionally fine window has been preserved with a palm tree as its central motif (175). A Rococo doorway forms the entrance to a house on the Herengracht (173). The builders of old Amsterdam often produced amazing solutions in their endeavour to make every entrance different from the next. For example: a sailing ship in a Rococo frame on the Singel (177), a copper mill on the Keizersgracht (178) and female figures supporting a balcony (a rarity in Amsterdam), also on the Keizersgracht (179). A remarkable and well-preserved relief decorating the

177

178

179

180

181

182

169 Hoisting-beams on 240-242 Keizers-
gracht. 170 Spout gable with hoisting-
beam, 100 Westerstraat. 171-172 Hoist-
ing-beams on 95 Leidsegracht and 186
Singel. 173 60 Herengracht. 174-175
19-21 Rusland. 176 284 Nieuwezijds
Voorburgwal. 177 36 Singel. 178
255 Keizersgracht. 179 539 Keizers-·
gracht. 180 136 Oudezijds Voorburg-
wal. 181 39 Oude Schans. 182 65
Kloveniersburgwal.

doorway of a house on the Oudezijds
Voorburgwal shows Admiral Cornelis
Maartenszoon Tromp in full regalia
(180). The scene is taken from the
Battle of Kijkduin, south of Den
Helder, in which De Ruyter and
Tromp, reconciled after years of
enmity, frustrated an Anglo-French
fleet's attempt to land in North
Holland. On a house on the Oude
Schans (181) two coopers are at work
on doors that have been brought from
some building undergoing restoration.
An allegorical female figure decorates
a house on the Kloveniersburgwal
(182). An earlier generation painted
these reliefs white, but there is a
growing tendency nowadays to prefer
the old practice of using colours.

Stories from gable stones

183

ABRAHAM

184

Amsterdam still possesses a great number of gable stones. These practical façade decorations were often used by the former inhabitants to proclaim their profession, origins, faith or what have you. Many of the stones are of a religious nature, for example that in Oudezijds Achterburgwal (183) depicting the famous words of Luther inspired by Psalm 18, verse 3. In the Begijnhof Abraham shows his willingness to sacrifice Isaac (184), an angel descending just in time to prevent him from doing so. In the Bethaniënstraat (185) a passage from Acts is quoted.

185

In old photographs one can still see the market crowds on the Singel near the Spui, which was once the site of a fruit market known, after the manner of bygone days, as the 'apple market'. It is not so surprising, therefore, that one of the houses on the Singel should have a gable stone portraying the crucial moment in the story of Adam and Eve, namely that at which Eve, prompted by a serpent coiled in the tree, takes the apple and offers it to Adam (186). A lion looks on. A careful examination of this animal tempts one to assert that – in contrast to the many others of its breed in

186

187

188

189

193

190

191

192

foreign towns and regions are to be found on many gable stones. One house in Monnikenstraat (191) bears the name 'De stat Wesel' (The City of Wesel), while another on the opposite side displays 'De Stat Oldenburg' (City of Oldenburg). A house on the Keizersgracht has a view of a city of many towers with tall ships, representing Bordeaux (199). On the same canal one can see houses and towers belonging to the seigneurie of Udinck (196) and on N.Z. Kolk a gilded half moon. Castles and citadels are also fairly common, examples being Egmont Castle (189), one whose identity is unknown (190) and a tower of Malaga Castle on the Bloemgracht keeping alive the memory of Amsterdam's wine trade with this city (195). The principal figures of the well-known medieval tale of the struggle between

194

Amsterdam – this time it is not showing us the fiercest side of its nature. As this scene was on the coat of arms of the apple merchants' guild, the relationship between the stone and the site is clear beyond any doubt. Four crowned evangelists with their traditional attributes are found in a romantic setting in the Nieuwe Zijds Kolk (187). The Groenburgwal is a beautiful and well-preserved canal between the Amstel and the Raamgracht. If you look towards the city from the rustic drawbridge in Staalstraat your eye will be caught by the majestic tower of the Zuiderkerk, one of Hendrick de Keyser's many creations.

Among the houses worth looking at along the canal there is one that originally boasted an early 17th century stepped gable but was given its present gable during later alterations. It is a well cared-for house with a lion's head at the top and in the middle a gable stone on which Hercules displays his strength (188). Though not a masterpiece of architecture, it is one of the many houses that help to make Amsterdam the wonderful city it is. Names and pictures of Dutch and

Charlemagne and the 'Four Sons of Aymon' – Adelaert, Ritsaert, Writsaert and Renout – also live on in Amsterdam. With the help of their magic steed Beyaert the children managed to escape to the Ardennes and finally to France. To such an extent was the story common property in the Middle Ages that numerous versions arose and were published as incunabula as early as c. 1490. Various old customs deriving from this story still survive, one of them being a procession with a huge version of the steed Beyaert in Dendermonde, in Belgium. The

195

196

197

198

story also provides the inspiration for a gable stone on the Herengracht, one of the most beautiful in Amsterdam, where for centuries now the four children have sat astride their black steed (197). A fine and rather unusual gable stone is to be seen on a house in Bloemstraat (192). The scrolls on each side indicate that the stone is over two hundred years old. The scene is a symbolic one with, on the left, the goddess Fame portrayed as a winged woman blowing a horn. On the right is a schoolmaster reading to his

199

200

201

202

audience – composed of a swan who does not seem very interested – out of a book with all the self-assurance of his age. Other allegorical scenes can be found on a house in Bloemstraat – 'Flora' (194) – and on one in Spuistraat (200). The latter bears the legend 'In 't Vlygende Kalf' (In the Flying Calf). A building on Nieuwezijds Voorburgwal (193) is called 'In den Wildeman', the portrait of the savage corresponding to its name being one of several in the city. The Nieuwezijds Kolk, busy section today, has a house with a stone, featuring a half moon and three stars.

The saying 'there is nothing new under the sun' has been overworked ever since Roman times. How true it is can be judged from a bylaw dated April 7, 1663, referring to traffic in Amsterdam. It was by no means the first and certainly not the last attempt to adapt to changed conditions. The city governors judged the streets and alleys of Amsterdam too narrow to accommodate 'state carriages and calashes'. They therefore decreed that, in order to prevent further accidents, state carriages and calashes would not be driven in or through the city either by residents or by non-residents. The only concession they were prepared to make was that anyone coming from outside the city should be allowed to drive straight to his house or lodgings – and vice versa in the case of a person leaving the city – provided always that he took the shortest route and avoided narrow streets

and alleys. It may be of some comfort to modern road-users to learn that the fine for breaking this bylaw was a hundred guilders, which in those days was a small fortune. Despite this, transgressions were sufficiently frequent that in 1669 it was decreed that the hundred guilder fine would apply not only to the user of the vehicle but also to its owner, irrespective of whether the latter had lent it or hired it out. This appears to have had some effect, but nine years later new measures had to be introduced. The ingenious device had been found of having vehicles made that did not qualify as state carriages or calashes.

They were small carriages with small wheels pulled by a single horse. Other new vehicles were given different names so that the ban on state carriages and calashes would not apply to them. A bylaw introduced in 1679 attempted to seal these loopholes. Apparently without complete success, because a new bylaw was passed in 1681 forbidding all persons whatsoever from driving in Amsterdam 'in state carriages, calashes, waggons, carts, gigs or any other vehicle, with four wheels or two or with runners'. Mail waggons and mail-coaches

203

were excepted and were even allowed to drive at a trot 'provided the necessary care is exercised'. It was not until 1736, many decades later, that driving was again allowed – for a price. Apparently the city governors had prohibited it not only for fear of accidents but also because of the wear and tear suffered by the streets. Street repairs were 'a heavy burden on the city's finances'. The city governors realized that it was time 'to make a reasonable concession to the convenience of the residents, specifically of those residents who keep state carriages, calashes, berlins, swimmers or other covered vehicles having a box at the front to seat a servant'. Not for nothing, however. Anyone who wanted to drive had to be prepared to hand over twenty-five guilders every year.

Whoever failed to do this fell under the old regulations and ran the risk of being fined 100 guilders. Only doctors of 45 years of age or over were exempted from the tax. Their younger colleagues had to pay the 'road tax' or walk. The city's traffic is depicted on numerous gable stones. That at number 7 Wijdesteeg (201) shows a passenger sledge that did not at first fall under the ban on 'state carriages and calashes'. In Nieuwe Zijdskolk a partially restored stone displays one of the mail-coaches which were permitted in the city provided they drove carefully (202). A colourful and in a certain sense historic gable stone on 74 Singel preserves the memory of the mail waggon and mail service to The Hague (203). This service, started in 1660, was the first from the capital and the main office was in this house on the Singel. Passengers were carried as well as mail. For a long time, however, the former preferred to travel by water. The journey took longer, but at least it was restful and allowed one to strike up a conversation and smoke one's Gouda pipe in peace. Many renderings of such scenes have survived.

204

205

206

207

208

210

gives an idea of the diversity of daily life. Tobacco products are fairly well represented on buildings. Among the finest gable stones – or rather, in this case, doorway decorations – is that on a house on the Geldersekade (208), showing a large barrel with tobacco leaves sticking out of it and two baskets with rolls of tobacco. The scenes are contained in a framework of late 18th century Rococo scrolls.

Cracknel has formed part of the pastrycook and confectioner's assortment for many centuries. This 'crackling' delicacy was originally baked by monks, who were used to hand it out to well-behaved children. The monks' interest in the product can perhaps be related to the view that in the cracknel's shape one can see a child with its arms folded across its chest. A very old cracknel gable stone is to be seen on a res-

209

A splendid 17th century ship embellishes a gable stone on the Prinsengracht (206) overlooking the bend opposite the Westerkerk. The ship, with its richly decorated stern, is a tall merchantman of the type used by the United East India Company, which in the 17th century carried spices and other exotic goods to Amsterdam from the rient. The ship is flying a large flag which still has its colours – red, white and blue. The sun with its abundant rays may symbolize the prosperity that the trade with the East brought to Amsterdam.

For a long time, fishing was even more important than the city's maritime trade. Both herring and whale were fished. The 'golden herring-boat' on the Singel recalls the flourishing herring-fishing industry (205). Three small rowing boats form the subject of a stone on the Amstel (207). The finest gable stone with a ship, however, is set in a wall on the Oudezijds Voorburgwal: a beautifully rigged vessel bearing the name "t Huyst vreest' with the date 1745 (204). High waves wash over the well-armed ship, a reminder of the glorious days of the Republic's fleet in the 17th century

Occupations are one of the most frequently occuring themes for gable stones. The great variety of occupations depicted on them

tored house in the St. Nicolaasstraat (210).

Restoration work in 1932 revealed the year 1564. The year 1932 was carved in the two rusks on either side of the cracknel.

It may seem surprising to find a farmer on a gable stone in the

211

heart of the old city. The man looks the passer-by straight in the eye and is shown ploughing his land with a disproportionately small horse. This gable stone on the Oude Waal (211), however, refers not to an occupation but to the name of the man who lived in the house: Joost Bouwer, who immortalized himself and his agricultural name with this stone. A portrait of a real farmer is still to be seen in the Eerste Looiersdwarsstraat. Here, a farmer from the Gooi region is displaying to the passer-by the fruits of his land (209).

In the Amsterdam of former times there were a great many hatters, making the small, large, flamboyant and highly serious hats that were worn then in such great numbers by men and women. Not so very long ago the last hatter's establishment closed its doors for the last time in the Korsjespoort-

steeg. A number of reminders of the city's hatters still survive. One of them is a gay red hat decorating a house on the Keizersgracht (216). On the Rozengracht a gable stone has survived of a maker of 'castor hats', hats made from beaver felt. On the Brouwersgracht lived a cabinetmaker who took his work very seriously and in 1759 compared the old-fashioned Dutch chair with the elegant French fauteuils which came into fashion in that period (215). A 'young carpenter' worked on the Egelantiersgracht (218), and in the Bethaniëndwarsstraat a fine stone (217) reminds us of a phenomenon that was also found in earlier days, that of the migrant worker; in this case, the grassmowers who came from Westphalia every year to cut grass. A cloth merchant displays his stacked goods on a façade in the St. Annendwarsstraat (212). Hendrick

Pieterszoon immortalized himself by having himself portrayed on a gable stone in the Bloemstraat (214) in the robes of his worthy office of undertaker's man – hat in one hand and notice of a death in the other. From a title-deed that has been preserved we know that Hendrick Pieterszoon bought the house in 1640. Thereafter it was known as the house 'with the undertaker's man on the front'. On the Lijnbaansgracht is one of the many gable stones that are based on a legend. The stone (213) shows a man's boot – a heavy boot with a black foot and red top, with

a double eagle on the side and a golden crown on top. The text reads: 'In the crowned emperor's boot'. The reference is to a story said to have taken place in Brussels in the 9th century, in which Emperor Charlemagne was involved. The wife of a bootmaker bought a chicken at the market. The emperor, who happened to be watching her, fancied the chicken

219

himself. He had the woman followed and that same evening went to the bootmaker's house and asked him to mend his boot. The bootmaker was more interested in his chicken, which was already roasting, than in mending boots and refused. The emperor, however, sent his servant to fetch wine. The bootmaker liked that idea better and invited the emperor – who, of course, had not made himself known – to join him at table. Apparently it was a pleasant evening. The emperor summoned the unsuspecting bootmaker to court the next day, and the latter was astonished to discover who his guest of the previous evening had been. The emperor asked how he could reward him, whereupon the man requested his permission to put a crowned boot in the coat of arms of the bootmakers' guild. The emperor agreed, and thus it was that many centuries later a bootmaker came to decorate his house with a stone that keeps the story alive.

Presumably there was not enough room for a projecting signboard in narrow Sint Nicolaasstraat, so the coffee merchant who, in the middle of the 18th century, wanted to draw attention to his business

220

decided on a gable stone. According to the assessment list the occupant of the house in the second quarter of the 18th century was one Johan Bont, a tea merchant. No doubt he would also sell coffee, being a related article, but this does not explain why he did not choose something having to do with tea for his gable stone (219). However that may be, the stone reminds us that in former days much of the coffee came from plantations in Surinam. The legend at the top reads 'The Surinam Coffee Barrel' and under it is a barrel, complete with bands, of the type used to transport the coffee. The barrel is open at one end and coffee beans are seen spilling out of it.

After the extension of the city in 1425 Amsterdam ended at the

Singel, which in those days was partly made up of the Kloveniersburgwal and Geldersekade. The total length was roughly 3,000 metres. The fact that the Singel was the site of the city wall until after 1600 is preserved in such names as Torensteeg (Tower Alley, the tower in this case being that of the Jan Rooden Gate) and Korsjespoortsteeg. Other indications that the Singel was once the city limit include a gable stone showing the Hague mail-coach and one showing a mill, the De Roo Oly Molen (222). Mail-coaches

221

stopped at the city limit, while mills were usually located on or near the city wall.

One of the best-known portrayals of early Amsterdam is that by Cornelis Anthonieszoon, a painter who died in 1554. The man who commissioned this painting of the city, Emperor Charles V, never saw it, but a visitor to the Historical Museum will find it preserved in all its glory. It shows Amsterdam – still a small city then – in detail, like a precursor of our aerial photographs or three-dimensional maps. Anthonieszoon lived behind the Nieuwe Kerk, in the 'Schrijvende hand' (Writing hand), where Amsterdammers

222

could purchase prints of wood engravings scrupulously carved by Anthonieszoon in twelve blocks. A house in Egelantiersstraat next to the entrance to Anslo's almshouse has a similar gable stone, showing a crowned quill. The stone preserves the memory of the schoolmaster Hendrick Wien, who lived there in the first half of the 16th century (220).

Amsterdam has many reminders of the national naval hero Michiel Adriaenszoon de Ruyter, the lieutenant-admiral who commanded the republic's fleet in many a sea battle and was responsible for some of the greatest achievements in our maritime history. De Ruyter settled in Amsterdam in 1653. Later he went to live on the Nieuwe Waalseiland on the Buitenkant (Outside), the present Prins Hendrikkade, whence he could survey the harbour where his and other fleets lay at anchor in all their picturesque splendour. De Ruyter bought the house in 1661 for a little over 28,000 guilders. No doubt it was often the scene of tributes and festivities when De Ruyter returned home after a victory, but it was also the focal point on 'mad Tuesday', September 6, 1672, when a mob advanced on the house to plunder it in the belief that, in those sombre days of a year of diasaster, De Ruyter

224

De Ruyter was set in the façade c. 1829 (224). Lying at anchor above the door are some beautifully rigged ships – sails billowing and flags streaming in the wind – carved in wood. De Ruyter was made a Grootburger (Great Citizen) of Amsterdam, an exceptional honour which he shared with only one other man. He was killed in a battle with a French fleet off Sicily. His body was embalmed and brought to Amsterdam, where, after an impressive funeral (the long rows of mourners winding over the Dam have been preserved in old engravings), he was buried in the Nieuwe Kerk. Rombout Verhulst made his splendid mausoleum, which once more gloriously embellishes the church.

One of the well-known inhabitants of 17th century Amsterdam was Jan Swammerdam (1637-1680), whose father, in addition to an apothecary, had a collection of curiosities which achieved some fame in its day. The building on the Oude Schans still exists and boasts a gable stone with the words: 'Jan Swammerdam 1637-1680. His investigations of nature will remain an example to all ages' (223). The text refers to the pioneering work he did in the study of insects, which he classified in a new way, based in part on the investigations he carried out in the polder country around Amsterdam. Swammerdam had a difficult life, and during one period was deeply under the influence of Antoinette

de Bourignon de la Porte, a fanatic who believed she had been called to proclaim a new Christianity and regarded herself as a second Eve or Mary. Because of her he stopped with his scientific work and even considered destroying his manuscripts. Finally he bequeathed them to the French natural scientist Thevenot. Fifty years later they were bought and published by Boerhaave, a physician in Leiden. They became known under the title 'Bible of Nature'. Another memorial to him is to be seen in the church in which he is buried, the Walenkerk on Oude Zijds Achterburgwal, where his name is inscribed on a pillar.

Another well-known Amsterdammer is commemorated by a stone in the narrow Koestraat. In this

223

had betrayed the fleet to the French. Inhabitants of the district, supported by musketeers, pikemen and other types of soldiers of the day, succeeded in subduing the riots and the mob was finally dispersed. According to the celebrated historian of Amsterdam, Jan Wagenaar, in this same period someone also forced his way into the house and tried to murder the admiral. A portrait of

225

226

230

street was the home and workshop, set up in a former monastery chapel, of Jan van der Heyden, the inventive father of such things as the fire engine fitted with a hose and the lamp-post (225). Van der Heyden's ideas were also adopted abroad, in part because of the marketing campaigns he undertook in neighbouring countries, using large posters. Many works in the Rijksmuseum show his great merit as a painter. An example of the cityscapes in which he specialized is his lively portrayal of the Dam with the Town Hall and the Nieuwe Kerk. The publishing house Elsevier kept up a tradition by placing the Elsevier family's publisher's trademark, which has been in existence since 1584, above the entrance to its building on the Spuistraat. The site of Daniël Elsevier's house on the Damrak is marked by a plaque of the type placed each year on eligible

houses by the Winkler Prins Foundation on Amsterdam's 'birthday', October 27th.
The early inhabitants of Amsterdam had a much closer association with animals than those of today. Most of them had horses, cows, pigs, sheep or poultry somewhere in a shed or stable at home or in the district. This may explain why so many gable stones show animals that are nowadays found only in the countryside, on farms.

227

'T SCHAEP

In the Bloedstraat (Blood Street) a façade is crowned by a sheep giving milk to its lamb (226), accompanied by a text reading 'the giver of food is good'. The name of the street is derived from the fact that in the Middle Ages bloodletting was performed by monks here. A jumping ram in the St. Luciënsteeg comes straight out of the Bible (235). A young lamb is to be seen on the Prinsengracht (231), a spotted ox on the Prinsengracht (228) and in the Spuistraat (229). Another sheep decorates 293 Spuistraat (227).
A great many surnames in The Netherlands are derived from animals.
It is not surprising, therefore, that when builders were thinking of a subject for a gable stone they often decided on an animal.

228

ANNO 1661

D·BONTE OS

229

ANNO 1695

Conversely, later occupants often adopted the name of the house. The stone on the Damrak showing a cock does not owe its existence to the multitude of cocks that could be heard crowing in the city in former times, but is probably a reference to the name of an occupant, Hendrick Hancock, who dealt in groceries here in the first half of the 18th century (230). One explanation of the stone, though it has not gone unchallenged, is that the hand and the cock represent a somewhat free interpretation of the name. Probably the occupant came from England. In America there are many memorials to John Hancock, who in 1776 was chairman of the meeting that declared the independence of what was to become the United States of America. Among other things, one of the most remarkable buildings in Chicago is named after him. The street scenes of earlier days were no less lively than those of modern shopping streets. In

232

231

233

particular, signboards in a variety of shapes and colours, many of them with paintings and some of them with very fine ones, informed the passer-by where he could buy shoes, clothes, bread, books and many other articles. Almost all of the signboards have disappeared. Existing signs with some history behind them are the yawning men, of which·a great number are still to be seen in both

234

the old and the new city. Preserved in the Warmoestraat is the head of an ox (233), formerly used to indicate the presence of a leather or hide merchant, or sometimes a butcher's. The ox wreathed with flowers on the Nieuwendijk (234) is a reminder of the days when, with festive display, the guild ox was led to the spit at a banquet of the Civic Guard – just as in ancient Rome an animal bedecked with flowers was led to the slaughter-block as an offering to the gods.
Gable stones can be found even in the smallest streets. Anyone who can find the Gordijnensteeg (232) – a side street of a side street of Oude Zijds Achterburgwal – will notice high up on an unnumbered house in the narrowest part of the alley the stone 'In de Rooketel', dating from 1625. This shows an important domestic utensil of former days, namely a large pan

of the type that was hung above the fire.
Pieter Pieterszoon Heyn, known more familiarly in Dutch history as Piet Heyn, is thought to have lived in a house – now well-preserved and restored – in the Rapenburg (236), a narrow street that comes out on the broad stretch of water by 's-Gravenhekje and the Montelbaanstoren. The house is set off from the others in

235

236

237

Spanish fleet laden with silver in Matanzas Bay. The booty amounted to some fifteen million guilders, of which the shareholders of the West India Company got 50%. Heyn himself received 7,000 guilders and the sailors seventeen

238

the street by the powerful aura of the past that emanates from it: beautiful steps and door, a gable stone showing a frigate under full sail, artistically wrought cramp irons and a stone with 'Anno 1614' carved in old script. The centre of the façade is formed by wooden doors flanked by windows, above which are three arches resting on corbels. A gable with five steps completes the building. The house was built in 1614 by Frans Gerritszoon, a captain. By making his home here he was only a few hundred yards from the waterfront. Piet Heyn too would have looked for a house close to the roadstead where his ships lay. It may have been from this house that he set out for the Caribbean, where in 1628 he performed his celebrated exploit of capturing a

months' pay. The sailors considered this a meagre recompense and later tried to plunder the booty in Amsterdam. A gable stone in the Rozenstraat (239) commemorates the capture of the city of Salvador (Bahia) in Brazil. It shows four ships under fire from the cannons of the fort guarding the bay and has the Spanish name for the city under it: Bayad todos os sanctos. Though stones giving a date are not gable stones in the customary sense of the word, they contribute abundantly to the embellishment of façades. An example is the stone with an ornamental anchor on Oude Zijds Voorburgwal (238). One frequently used treatment of dates was to place them on elaborate cartouches. Above an entrance on the Waterlooplein (237) is a Jewish year 5638 (1878).

239

The Gates

Amsterdam is a city with many gateways and passages: entrances to buildings and the courtyards of almshouses
and narrow passageways between
houses. A narrow gateway next to
the Westerkerk (240) reminds us that
in former days people were buried
around as well as in churches. It gave
access to the West graveyard, which
continued in use up to the middle of
the 17th century, being replaced in
1655 by a new cemetery on a rampart

*240 Gateway beside the Westerkerk,
277b Prinsengracht. 241 Spinning
House entrance, Spinhuissteeg.
242 Decoration above the door of the
Wine Merchants' Guild in the Koestraat. 243 Entrance to the former
Rasp House, Heiligeweg.*

242

on the Bloemgracht. In the arch above
the gate are many of the traditional
symbols of cemeteries: a skull on a
pedestal flanked by four putti, the
outside one on the left resting on a
sand glass, the outside putto on the
right on a skull. The relief on the
pedestal showing a book and crossed
wind instruments was intended to
draw attention to the transient nature
of human existence. Many famous
people are buried inside the Wester-

241

243

244

245

kerk. One of the pillars has a memorial to Rembrandt, but where exactly in the church he was buried is not known. It is even possible that his mortal remains were later removed. Among the many others who were laid to rest here are Rembrandt's son Titus, the painter d'Hondecoeter, the engraver Romein de Hooghe, the cartographer and printer Joan Blaeu, Lucas Bols and Louis de Geer (the occupant of the House with the Heads).

Almost all the 17th century gateways are forceful structures with Baroque detail. Examples are the gateway of the former Spinhuis (Spinning House, a house of correction) in the Spinhuissteeg (241) and the Wine Merchants' guildhall in the Koestraat (242) with, above the entrance, Urbanus among the grapes. The gateway of the former

rasp house (house of correction) on the Heiligeweg includes a symbolic portrayal of punishment (243).

In the past as in the present, part of buildings were moved about to an incredible extent. An example is the gate of the municipal carpenter's yard in the Nieuwe Doelenstraat, which was given a number of beauty treatments before being moved to its present site on Oude Zijds Voorburgwal, where it forms the entrance to the Atheneum Illustre, Amsterdam's first university (244). This was originally the site of the Agnes monastery. With the Alteration, the transition to Calvinism, the monastery came into the possession of the city and some fifty years later was converted into a university. The chapel still exists and continues to be referred to by both

younger and older students as the Agnieten Chapel.

The gateway is a festive work, every inch Renaissance and provided with every type of curl and scroll in the repertoire of Vredeman de Vries from Leeuwarden. The rounded arch is richly ornamented with lion's heads, stone rings (a reminder of the iron rings in walls for tethering horses) and other motifs (249). Surmounting the gateway is one of the most ornate examples of Amsterdam's coat of arms, with exuberantly imaginative cartouches and vases framing and doing honour to the three St. Andrew's crosses.

The date, however, has been tampered with. The original date, 1571, was covered over with putty and a new one, 1631, substituted.

246

the one and 'Brakke Grond' (Brackish Land) the other.

For the occupants of the monasteries that stood here in the 15th century, penetration of Zuiderzee water had the unfortunate consequence that the water in the monasteries' wells also became brackish and was no longer fit for drinking. As far as the city's architecture is concerned, the only thing of importance is the beautiful gateway next to the Enge Lombardsteeg that continues to embellish Oude Zijds Voorburgwal. The gateway's two pilasters are ornate at the bottom and severe at the top, where they encounter a crossbeam decorated

with two lion's heads. The pilasters display two cherub's heads (246) of a type which one would expect to find on an Italian palazzo rather than beside an Amsterdam canal. From above the arch the observer finds himself under the terrible gaze of a lion's head. The date shown is 1624, but as in the case of many other gateways there is reason to treat it with suspicion and assume an older date. The Kalverstraat boasts one of the oldest gates, that of the former City Orphanage, dating from 1581, with the orphans in the city's colours (see 5) and the lines by Joost van den Vondel beneath.

Formerly, where the fresh water of the Amstel and the salt water of the Zuiderzee met and mixed the result was brackish water. As a deposit of sand, or 'nes', formed, the site came to be known as the Nes. This explains two names familiar to Amsterdammers and non-Amsterdammers alike, 'Nes'

244 Agnietenpoort, Oudezijds Voorburgwal. 245 Brakke Grond gate, Oudezijds Voorburgwal. 246 Detail of Brakke Grond gate. 247 Binnengasthuis gate, Grimburgwal. 248 Detail of gate of former City Orphanage, 92 Kalverstraat. 249 Detail of Agnietenpoort, Oudezijds Voorburgwal.

247

248

249

250

looters and thieves were at work while the building was still ablaze, which suggests that the immediate vicinity sheltered a great many citizens of the light-fingered variety. Members of the audience fleeing from the theatre were relieved of their jewelry, and thieves were already at work in the commissioners' room when they were surprised by fire-fighters.

The theatre was not rebuilt on the same spot but removed to the Leidseplein, where it underwent the same fate in 1890. A few years later a new theatre was opened, the Stadsschouwburg (City Theatre), which continues to be the city's theatrical focal point. Inscriptions in the courtyard of the original building, which now houses offices, record its former function as a theatre. An interesting feature are

The gate of the Agnes Chapel and that of the Historical Museum in the St. Luciënsteeg (250) have the same provenance: they were removed from the municipal carpenter's yard in the Nieuwe Doelenstraat and re-erected at separate sites. The gate in the St. Luciënsteeg was installed at its present site in 1634 as the entrance to the Girls' Orphanage, built by Van Campen, which has now become the Amsterdam Historical Museum. The City Orphanage gate is not as richly ornamented as that on Oudezijds Voorburgwal but it has the same scroll-work characteristic of Vredeman de Vries. Here too the builders removed the old date and substituted 1634, the year in which it was removed and put to its new use. On the Keizersgracht, enclosing a small forecourt, is the entrance gate to the Nederduitse Schouwburg (Low German Theatre). On the evening of May 11, 1772, this was the scene of one of the biggest fires in Amsterdam's history. According to tradition, the glow could be seen as far away as Texel and in other parts of the city there was enough light to tell the time on the tower clocks.

The gate is the work of Jacob van Campen and in former days displayed the celebrated lines of Joost van den Vondel: 'De wereld is een speeltoneel,

Elk speelt zijn rol en krijgt zijn deel' (The world is a stage, Each plays his part and receives his portion). The stories about this fire make interesting reading. The fire was caused by overheating resulting from the use of extra lights for a performance of 'De Qualyk bewaarde dogter'. Understandably, panic broke out.

Among the seventeen people who lost their lives was the well-known architect Cornelis Rauws, who had built the Muiderpoort a few years earlier. The accounts contain the surprising information that a large number of

252

251

the large bread ovens, which have been preserved and now form part of one of the main rooms.

Unfair as it may be to the female occupants of former days, the beautiful gate (255) on Oudezijds Achterburgwal that provides access to the present university has been known for many a long year as the Oudemanhuispoort (Old Men's Home gate). The gate dates from the early years of the 17th century, at which time it formed the entrance to the Old Men's and Women's Home. In the days of historian Jan Wagenaar this held three times as many women as men. The gate links the canal with Kloveniersburgwal and has always been used as a public thoroughfare. The gate at

253

in the last century, making way, in 1879, for the main building of the Municipal University, its present function.

The gate of the Hofje De Star (254) on the Prinsengracht hides a great many house numbers. It is also known as the Van Brienenhofje, in memory of the founder, Arnout van Brienen, and his wife, who ran the almshouse in 1804. The entrance has a roof chapel with a small tower and dial.

At the top of the steps is an unused entrance with an arch framing two cherubs bearing a shield with a cross. The almshouse has twenty-one houses for Catholic pensioners, widows and widowers, arranged around a peaceful courtyard with a pump. In the Lombardsteeg is the gate of the Bank van Lening (251), through which Vondel passed for many years on his way to work.

the other end dates in its present form from 1786. The Oudemanhuispoort is small but very attractively designed: two Ionic half columns are surmounted by a semicircular arch flanked by decorative vases. A pair of spectacles are carved in the arch as a symbol of

the old people who lived there.
The space between the two gates has traditionally been occupied by small shops, where, already in the days of Wagenaar, 'there is a throng of buyers every day, and especially during the fairs'. The men and women disappeared

254

250 Upper part of the gate of the former City Orphanage, St. Luciënsteeg.
251 Gate of the Bank van Lening, Lombardsteeg. 252 Gate of a former theatre at 384 Keizersgracht.
253 Group by B.W.H. Ziesenis (1792) on the façade of the Evangelische Lutherse Kerk, Kloveniersburgwal.
254 Upper part of the entrance gate of the Van Brienenhofje on the Prinsengracht. 255 Oudemanhuispoort on Oudezijds Achterburgwal.

256

T'GELOOF.

257

DE GLOYENDE OVEN

258

259

The Almshouses

Prosperity enough in the Amsterdam of the Golden Age, but also poverty and fear of old age. Those who had sufficient wealth to do so and took their faith seriously founded an alms-house for widows and the elderly. The oldest of Amsterdam's almshouses is the Begijnhof, which goes back to the Middle Ages and in the present century forms a remarkable oasis in the city (256-259). The Begijnhof provides homes for Roman Catholic women. A courtyard in the heart of Amsterdam with beautiful houses, gable stones and two churches, telling a tale of piety, repentance and faith (257-258). The Begijnhof's original church is the one resembling a village church, which was consecrated in 1419. A painting by an unknown artist shows us that little has changed in the course of a few hundred years (256). After falling into disuse fol-lowing the Reformation and standing empty for many years, in 1607 the church was given to English and Scottish Presbyterians, who did not wish to become members of the Episcopal Church. To this day it has remained the English Reformed Church. During the German occupation the building was consequently appropriated as enemy property and used by the German Wehrmacht. The church contains the grave of the Italian musician Pietro Antonio Locatelli (1695-1764), who won part of his fame during the many years in which he lived in Amsterdam, at 506 Prinsengracht.

The Reformation deprived the Catholics of their original Begijnhof church and it was not until 1671 that they secured a new place of worship by constructing a clandestine church in two adjoining houses. This church became the centre for the procession of the Miracle, which, as the 'Silent Procession', has become a Catholic tradition. It has been kept up since 1881 and still makes its way through nocturnal Amsterdam in March of

260

261

every year. Only men are allowed to take part in the procession, which follows an old procession route and takes place in silence and without any form of outward display. This annual event commemorates a miracle which occurred in 1345: according to records of the day a sick man vomited out a consecrated wafer and it remained floating in the fire. A large painting shows the procession as it was in former days, making its way through the streets of the city centre. Almost twenty of the houses in the Begijnhof still have parts of their medieval wooden frame. The almshouse also has one of Amsterdam's two surviving wooden houses, which underwent restoration in the 1950s. Behind a splendid façade on the Prinsengracht, the Protestant almshouse Deutzenhof (261). Formerly – and even now – to obtain a place in it was to be fortunate indeed. The Deutzenhofje is perhaps the most distinguished of Amsterdam's almshouses. It was founded by Agneta Deutz (1663-1692), who disinherited her son because of misbehaviour and decided to leave her wealth to charity. The almshouse was built after her death in 1694 by Pieter de Zeeuw. The entrance on the canal is beautifully decorated, displaying among other things the coat of arms of Agneta Deutz and her two husbands. The courtyard has a large pump and is enclosed by twenty houses and a hall with Doric columns. One of the most

celebrated inhabitants was Henriëtte de Nerha (1754-1818), who had been Mirabeau's mistress in Paris before he fled to Amsterdam and took up residence in the Sint Luciënsteeg. The French politician's sojourn is commemorated by a plaque placed by the Winkler Prins Foundation on the house where he lived.

On the Nieuwe Keizersgracht is the Van Brants Rushofje, built by Daniël Marot. The almshouse was founded by Christoffel Brants, a wealthy merchant who traded chiefly with Russia. The entrance and the courtyard (260) have been preserved in their original state, as has the governors' room (262), whose view over the garden takes the visitor back in time to another age. Through his trade with Russia, Christoffel Brants developed a friendship with Czar Peter the Great, who stayed at Brants' house at 317 Keizersgracht on his second visit to Amsterdam. Brants' birthday is still celebrated every year in the almshouse.

Occo's Hof, also on the Nieuwe Keizers-

262

256 The Begijnhof on a painting by an unknown artist. 257-258 Gable stones in the Begijnhof. 259 Houses in the Begijnhof. 260, 262 Pump and Governors' Room in the Van Brandts Rushofje, 38-44 Nieuwe Keizersgracht. 261 Entrance of the Deutzenhof, 857-897 Prinsengracht.

gracht, has the dignified air of a French monastery. Much more intimate is the almshouse founded by the Grill family in the Eerste Weteringdwarsstraat, the atmosphere of whose houses recalls the everyday life of a bygone age. Small though the Grillhofje is, it is impossible to pass this peaceful spot without at least looking up at its nine bell gables, which have been beautifully restored and are too striking to be resisted.

The façades are identical aside from a break in the pattern in the middle of the row and face onto a small by-street of their own which receives but little light in the winter months (263). The visitor reaches the almshouse by means of a narrow passage which opens out onto the by-street. An old

clock, which has been there longer than anyone can remember, ticks away the time for the small community that inhabits the houses (264). Grill's Hofje owes its existence to the benevolence of Antonie Grill, a silversmith who died in 1727 and had the houses built for women of the Reformed or Lutheran faith over sixty years of age. This initiative of the Grills is recorded with a moral attached in a poem in the governors' room:
'Anthony Grill, die met zijne echtgenoot/Mij heeft gestigt, leert ons nog na hun dood,/Hoe ieder lid der Christelijke Kerke/Dient zijn geloof te toonen door zijne werke.'
(Anthony Grill, who founded me together with his wife, continues to teach us after their death that every

member of the Christian Church should show his faith trough his work.)

Also in the Eerste Weteringdwarsstraat, at the Vijzelstraat end, is the Hodshon-Dedelshofje, which was founded in 1842 by Isaac Hodshon and Isabella Dedel. A gate in a long wall gives access to a courtyard, around three sides of which are the dwellings. The houses are built in the not very

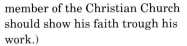

265

263

266

joyful style of the mid-19th century, but the courtyard is brightened up by a freestone pump crowned by an ornate lamp.

Many more almshouses are tucked away in the narrow streets of the Jordaan. In general they are plainer than those elsewhere in the city. In the Egelantiersstraat is what used to be Anslo's Hofje, which was founded in the years 1615-1616 by Claes Claesz., a Mennonite. It was extended a number of times, but after the Second World War became uninhabited and fell into a state of advanced decay. A foundation was created to save it and had it restored, since which time its atmosphere of peace and intimacy

264

by means of a narrow passage running between the houses. The Van Brienenhofje was founded in 1804 by Arnout Jan van Brienen and his wife. Zon's Hofje, a few doors further, was founded originally for Mennonite widows but is now occupied by female students. A gable stone showing Noah's Ark, an appropriately edifying text and a sundial continue to form an attractive detail on one of the walls (268).

267

268

269

has made it a much sought-after residence notably for artistically-inclined young people. A building next to the almshouse was inhabited in the 17th century by the schoolmaster Hendrick Theunisz. Wient, whose gable stone still adorns it. Other almshouses in the vicinity are the Regenboogliefdehofje and the Hofje van de Zeven Keurvorsten (Almshouse of the Seven Electors).

On the Palmgracht one finds the Hofje van Raep (267), which has been converted into private housing. The 'raap' (turnip) depicted above the gate relates to the name of the founder, Pieter Adriaenszoon Raep, who lived from 1581 to 1666 and founded the almshouse in 1648. Its establishment is memorialized by the Raeps' coat of arms on the façade and the date 1648

(269). Another Raep, Pieter Raep, a son of Adriaen Pieterszoon, lived on the Dam. Pieter Raep must have known Joost van den Vondel; at any rate he composed the lines which are still to be seen above the entrance to the almshouse:

'Pieter Raep, de Trezorier
Boude uit mededogen hier
't Weduwen- en Weezenhof
Men gebruike het tot Godts lof'
(Out of compassion Pieter Raep, the Thesaurer, built here the Widows' and Orphans' Court. May it be used in God's praise).

There are two almshouses at the beginning of the Prinsengracht. One of them is the Catholic almshouse De Star, better known as the Van Brienenhofje, and is closed off by a gate; the other, Zon's Hofje, is reached

263-264 Lane and clock outside the Grillhofje, 11-43 Eerste Weteringdwarsstraat. 265-266 Gable stone and pump in Anslo's Hofje, 50 Egelantiersstraat. 267 Hofje van Raep, with gable stone (269), 28-38 Palmgracht.
268 Sundial in Zon's Hofje, 175 Prinsengracht.

The Townhall on Dam Square

The town hall on the Dam was designed c.1640 by Jacob van Campen. In 1648, the year of the treaty that put an end to the eighty years' war of liberation from Spain and finally brought peace to the Republic, the decision was made to go ahead with building. By that time a start had already been made on sinking the 13,659 piles that were needed. After many quarrels and financial setbacks, the building was opened for use in 1655 and completed in 1662. For contemporaries this edifice was an incredibly impressive symbol of Amsterdam's might and wealth. The ornamentation – especially of the interior, with its marble, its sculptures and its paintings – was almost excessive by Dutch standards and did not fail to have the effect intended. It was a cool, classically inspired governors' palace of great stateliness, but one which nonetheless bowed to an old tradition by having a citizens' hall at its centre – a square in the heart of the building to which all citizens had free access. During the period of French rule the building housed Louis Bonaparte, brother of the French emperor. It has remained a palace ever since, but for the members of the House of Orange, Stadholders who saw their status raised after the Napoleonic era to that of kings. At present it is used by the Queen when she is in residence in the capital and by visiting heads of state. The virgin of peace (274) surmounts the façade's tympanum against the background of the dome containing the great carillon cast by Hemony. The vast triangle of the tympanum itself (275) shows the Virgin of the City holding the city's coat of arms, with a swirling group of tritons, sea nymphs and other allegorical persons and beasts paying homage to her. The work was executed by the Flemish sculptor Quellinus, who had come to Amsterdam with other artists to decorate the imposing new town hall. The statues of Justice and Caution (272-273) also date from the period when the building was a town hall. At the rear, Atlas raises the globe high above both the building and the bustle of the city (270). The large lamp-posts placed at the front and rear of the building (271) were the first to be used for gaslight. When it was found that the gas bills were extremely high, long deliberations were needed. The solution finally hit upon was to use smaller jets when

270

271

272

273

274

by the standards of our day the administration was very much a select club of rich and powerful gentlemen who got on together remarkably well. 'The Citizens' Hall is an imposing Room with a floor mosaic which is as striking as it is ambitious: the known world of those days and the celestial sphere, in marble and copper.

A town hall full of allegories of classical pedigree. Painted (279) and carved in stone (277, 278, 280). The large group (277) represents Justice, seated between Death and Punishment, treading Greed and Envy under foot. Above that is Atlas. The caryatid (280) is a beautiful detail in this building whose splendour is at its height in the great Citizens' Hall (278). The importance of the building, which Constantijn Huygens called the 'eighth wonder of the world' and of which Vondel wrote 'Van soo veel Steens om hoogh op soo veel Houts van onder/Van soo veel Kostelick so konstelick verwrocht' (Of so much stone above on so much wood below, of so much magnificence so artfully wrought), is underlined by the following quotation from Dr. F. Vermeulen: 'Thanks particularly to

270 The figure of Atlas at the rear of the Palace. 271 Lamp-post before the Palace, by Tetar van Elven. 272 Justice. 273 Caution. 274 The Virgin of Peace with tower in background. 275 Detail of the tympanum surmounting the façade. 276 (Overleaf). Painting by Gerrit Adriaensz. Berckheyde (1638-1698) showing an everyday scene on the Dam with the Town Hall on the left and on the right the Nieuwe Kerk and part of the Waag.

King William, who had had the lamps put there, was not in residence. A sufficient saving in gas consumption was thereby achieved that the bill was brought down to a level the city could afford.

Gerrit Adriaenszoon Berckheyde (1638-1698), who learnt the painter's craft from his brother Job and went on to become one of the most celebrated painters of realistic cityscapes, has given us a very clear idea of what the

town hall was like in its early days through his almost photographic rendering of it (276). The painting dates from only a few decades after the completion of the building, at which time the stone was still clean and the surroundings still intact. It can be seen from this work that not too much has changed in the course of over three centuries: the town hall still stands in all its splendour and little has happened to the New Church. The building on the right, however, failed to survive, for it was later demolished. For well over a century the city's affairs were regulated in this town hall, and especially in and around the citizens' hall, where anyone who wished could come to see and be seen. Arranged around the hall and the galleries were the administrative chambers, where only the city's governors were welcome – democratic it may all have been, and certainly was, by the standards of the day, but

275

the contribution made by Artus Quellien the Elder and his collaborators, this town hall is unquestionably the most brilliant and characteristic example, as well as one of the principal creations, of the classicistic Baroque not only in The

Netherlands but in the whole of Western Europe'.

It has been pointed out that the building's plan has a certain symbolic significance in that it resembles that of a medieval cathedral. The axis runs from west to east. At the east end, the part occupied by choir and altar in a church, was the Vierschaar, the place where justice was administered.

On the right side, often considered the best side, were the chambers of dignitaries such as the burgomaster and the treasurers. On the left were the Chamber of Justice, the Council Chamber and the chamber of the trustees charged with the care of orphans. The symmetry intended by the architect Van Campen was abandoned by his successor Daniël Stalpaert.

A few words might be in place here about a monument which for many years occupied a site on the Dam in front of the town hall – to many people's annoyance. Which Amster-dammer has not heard or seen old photographs of 'Naatje of the Dam'? It was placed in the centre of Dam Square in 1856 as a memorial to the 'spirit of 1830-1831', the time at which the protracted problems with Belgium began. The monument in the heart of Amsterdam failed, however, to win the hearts of Amsterdammers. It was designed by Tetar van Elven M. Gzn. and executed, strangely enough, by the Belgian Louis Royer. How little respect this work – towering to a height of almost eighteen metres above the Dam – commanded is illustrated by such nicknames as 'Miss Concord' and 'Naatje Concord'. The artist defended his design with a certain amount of vanity: 'Faithful to the laws given us by nature, the mistress of art, we have hoped to preserve such in our forms. Hence the broad foot, which makes the monument seem rooted in the ground, and also the slow and continuous diminution in the ascension so that it rises up tall to end in the image of Concord'. Others held a slightly different opinion. In the words of one critic: 'Naatje is a soulless accumulation of three lumps of stone, each forming a whole, which go together like the pieces of a Muscovite cake'. Moreover, an inferior sort of stone was used which was unable to stand up to the caprices of the Amsterdam climate. The monument soon lost its nose. This damage was repaired, but new misfortunes, the loss of an arm and persistent derision caused the authorities to have the work removed in 1914. Amsterdammers sang: 'Naatje of the Dam had to make way for the tram'.

The coming of the new town hall, a building which somewhat exceeded the proportions which had been preserved in the city thus far, drastically changed the appearance of the Dam. Anyone who has gone at all deeply into the matter of this building which represented the foundations of

277

278

277 Group of figures in the Citizens' Hall; above it, Atlas bearing the world on his shoulders. 278 The vast Citizens' Hall. 279 Many painters worked on the decoration; Rembrandt, whose work was not accepted, Jan Lievens, Ferdinand Bol, Thomas de Keyser, Jan Bronkhorst, Jacob Jordaens and numerous others. 280 Caryatid.

279

280

substructure completed. They considered it scandalous that fortunes should be spent on a secular building while God's house had to do without a tower. The fire, however, made it necessary to set aside such differences and act, and thus it was that priority was finally given to finishing the new town hall. Later, attempts to complete the tower were to be frustrated for a second time, the decisive factor on this occasion being the war with England. To the present day, the tower remains unbuilt.

Before work on the new town hall could begin a large number of houses had to be pulled down, many of them bearing such splendid names as 'The Sultan', 'The Spectacles' and 'The Butter Tub of France'. Another building on the Dam, the Waag (Weighhouse), still had another century and a half of life before it. One can get a good idea of what it looked like in its original form by visiting a building which resembles it, the Weigh-house which continues to embellish the centre of the city of Hoorn. The Waag was used to house the city guard as well as for the weighing of goods. For the latter purpose, the doors were furnished with seven large scales, in addition to which there were a number of small scales for weighing costly goods such as silk and indigo.

Amsterdam's and even the Republic's power will be astonished that noble works can be undertaken in such sorry surroundings. The former, medieval town hall, preserved forever by numerous painters but especially by Pieter Janszoon Saenredam (1597-1665), is usually portrayed as a romantic, rather dilapidated building, inevitably embellished by a whale's jaw.

On the Dam side the town hall that was built in 1393 had a gallery with a three-arched arcade surmounted by three elaborately ornamented Gothic windows. Next to it stood a slender tower. In the course of time, however, the tower began to evince such signs of sinkage that in 1601 the city carpenter had to apply all his arts to the matter of righting it. This proved to be only a temporary solution, and fifteen years later the spire had to be demolished. The city bells finished up on the flat-topped, truncated tower, but later this in turn fell victim to decay and disappeared. It is difficult to imagine where the city fathers of those days actually met, because in addition to being a town hall the building housed a discount bank, a court of justice, an inspection hall for cloth and a cellar in which prisoners were fastened to the walls. The decision, therefore, to build a new town hall was no needless extravagance, and when the old town hall burned to the ground in 1652 the necessity became even greater. Surviving engravings and paintings show the commotion on the square during the fire, with men hurrying hither and thither, a large body of spectators being kept back by guards and dozens of fire-fighters passing buckets of water from hand to hand. Yet others are climbing ladders with buckets of water in an effort to save the building, but the flames shooting out of every part of it and licking the truncated tower were to prove victorious.

As far as the controversy around the building of a replacement was concerned, the fire was decisive. We saw earlier how bitter the struggle was which had arisen between administrators and clergymen. The latter did everything in their power to bring about the completion of a high tower for the New Church, the piles for which had already been sunk and the

281

Though the building eventually lost its original function it would probably be gracing the Dam to the present day were it not for the fact that Louis Bonaparte, who took possession of the town hall in 1808 and converted it into a palace, decided to have the building pulled down because it spoilt his view. After the withdrawal of the French, Amsterdam continued to be deprived of the use of the luxurious building as its town hall. In 1873, however, a number of inhabitants sent a petition to the town council requesting that the Palace be given back to the city. This was the start of the 'Palace-Town Hall question', which still – over a century later – has not

281, 605 Herengracht is a double-fronted house which was built in 1686-1687 and owned in the 19th century by the Willet-Holthuysen who bequeathed the house to the city. It is now furnished as an 18th century canal house. In addition to period rooms it also has a garden laid out in the 18th century manner complete with statues. 282 Garden house reassembled behind the Rijksmuseum.

been resolved in all its implications. In 1935 the city of Amsterdam concluded an agreement with the State whereby Amsterdam relinquished its rights to the building in return for a payment by the State of ten million guilders to enable the capital to build a new town hall. This in turn gave rise to the 'Town Hall question',

which, again, has still not been resolved almost fifty years later. A site was selected for the new town hall; competitions were organized to choose a design and a design was duly chosen; but, every time, execution of the work proved impossible. In 1978-1979 the site was even cleared for building by pulling down numerous existing buildings and moving the traditional Waterloo Square market to another location. Meanwhile, costs have risen to a multiple of the original estimate of ten million guilders, and for this reason the most recent plans combine the town hall with an opera house. The battle on this issue is not yet over, so for some years to come Amsterdam will no doubt have to continue to make do with housing its municipal administration in the Prinsenhof.

No parks or public gardens in the old part of Amsterdam, but an aerial photograph reveals a remarkable amount of greenery. With the exception of the elms along the canals, however, the greenery is behind the houses and the private domain of their owners. Every occupant of a house on the canals had a long, narrow garden at the back, which was laid out as a pleasure ground. A typical city garden of two centuries ago can be seen in a painting by Cornelis Troost (284) in the Rijksmuseum. Despite its limited

282

size its owner has endeavoured to squeeze in all of the features found in a royal park, but in miniature: statues, pergola, summerhouse, sundial, trees, flowers, even a grapevine. Safely closed-in, intimate, a part of the house and not by any means a place for the children to romp about in, because everything is as meticulously cared for here as in the house itself. Cornelis Troost was one of the most gifted painters of the 18th century and aside from this portrait of an Amsterdam garden has left us many

places. In the gardens of the Rijksmuseum (282) one finds a garden house belonging to a vanished building from which one can get some idea of the size and the wealth of ornament that such structures could attain. Photograph 283 shows a detail of a city garden with a stone arbour in the shade of large chestnut trees, facing towards the rear of the house. More care is being taken of these old gardens nowadays and there are regulations preventing them from being swallowed up by extensions or con-

verted into car parks. The patrician house Willet-Holthuysen was made into a museum in 1895 and is a fine example of a stately home which has been preserved intact. A few years ago the banking house next to it donated sufficient funds to enable the garden (281, 289, 291) to be completely restored in the style of a Dutch Baroque garden, with the flower beds and statues characteristic of 18th century Holland. Needless to say, this was a priceless assignment for garden historians, and they have acquitted

283

other records of the life led by his contemporaries. He has sometimes been compared with William Hogarth, the English genre painter and portraitist whose work, like that of Troost, excels through its impartiality and fresh colours. Many of these gardens behind the houses along Amsterdam's canals are well worth seeing. In the past, and occasionally even now, the gardens had to make way for extensions housing offices, but pleasure grounds such as the one portrayed by Troost are still to be found in many

283 Sundial in the garden behind 517 Keizersgracht. 284 Painting by Cornelis Troost (1697-1750) showing what for many 18th century Amsterdammers was the ideal garden.

284

285

287

286

288

themselves admirably. As the building beyond the end of the garden, on the Amstelstraat, has been pulled down, the garden is now visible from that street and thus unique in Amsterdam. The building that is now the Willet-Holthuysen Museum and is fitted out as a canal palace of 18th century Amsterdam was constructed in 1686 for a former ambassador to various foreign courts. In the 19th century the house was occupied by one Abraham Willet and his wife Sandrina Louise Geertruide Holthuysen, who caused their names to live on after them by leaving the house together with the library and art collection to the city of Amsterdam. Though the first concern of Amsterdammers was with the practical utility and embellishment of their houses, already in the 17th century interest arose in the laying out of gardens, as can be seen from Meerhuizen, a country seat on the Amstel built in 1614. In 1668 a book appeared in Amsterdam addressed 'To the Gardener', which contained a great many examples and, among other things, 200 models for the construction of arbours, mazes and sundials. The Dutch country gardens were heavily influenced by the Renaissance, the Baroque and the Rococo but attained a certain indivi-duality through enclosure by ditches and the division into squares in which different types of gardens were laid out. A typical feature of both the country gardens and those in Amsterdam was the 'teahouse', in whose peaceful atmosphere tea was taken at midday. In the 17th century the first tulips

285, 288, 290 Entrance and statues in Frankendael. 286 Garden of Brants Rushofje, 38-40 Nieuwe Keizersgracht. 287 Coachhouse behind 524 Keizersgracht. 289, 291 Statues in Garden of Willet Holthuysen Museum.

and hyacinths began to make their appearance in the city gardens. At first these plants, which came to the Republic from Turkey and were to play such an important part in the areas to the southwest of Amsterdam, were expensive and rare. Here and there, plants from the Far East flourished, having been carried back to Holland aboard spice-laden East-Indiamen. It was not only the lack of space in the city which prevented horticulture from developing on a grander scale. It was also that the absence of a court such as one had in France and England meant that – in contrast to those countries – no really ambitious projects were undertaken. The suburb of Amsterdam known as Watergraafsmeer was once the real lake that its name suggests, located outside the city. It was later drained and used by wealthy Amsterdammers for building country houses. Enormous sums were sometimes spent on these castle-like seats with their extensive gardens. Quite a few country houses have survived, but the only one to have been preserved in Watergraafsmeer is Frankendael: a good example of an average country house, not extravagantly luxurious but provided nonetheless with gates, statues, waterworks and outbuildings. The very picture of pleasant, relaxed living (285, 288, 290).

From the garden behind 524 Keizersgracht one has a view of the wall of the coach-house of 61 Kerkstraat, with statues of Ceres and Hercules (287). A sedate garden (286) behind the Van Brants Rushofje.

290

289

291

The Museums

What one might call Amsterdam's 'best room' is no longer in the heart of the city but just beyond the southern edge of the old part, in the form of the Rijksmuseum on Museum Square. The Rijksmuseum was opened in 1885 and aside from being the largest and most visited museum in Holland is one of the best-known art galleries in the

292 The towers of the Rijksmuseum. 293 Detail showing the variety of the masonry. 294 View from the arcade at the back of the Rijksmuseum.

world. Like the Uffizi in Florence it is primarily a museum of national rather than international art, and houses an excellent collection of the former. In many respects Amsterdam's art epitomizes national art, for its status of capital extends also, and perhaps above all, to the field of culture. The building itself is a perfect example of the neo-Gothic style of the last century and its designer, Pierre Cuypers, was the best architect of his day. Though it is scarcely typical of Amsterdam, it is unquestionably a building with some character. The Rijksmuseum heads a list of thirty-five museums of various sizes and types to be found in Amsterdam. Of

292

293

294

295

museum also exhibits other modern art. The Historical Museum's beautifully housed collection furnishes a comprehensive history of the city of Amsterdam.

As the capital of The Netherlands, Amsterdam is the country's leading cultural centre. It has two universities. It also has a musical life which has been made known in other part of the world through the medium of the Concertgebouworkest (Concert Hall Orchestra).

In the Low Countries there has always been a close link between economic life and cultural life: when the economy flourished, culture flourished. One of the clearest examples of this is the Republic's Golden Age. Of the various cultural spheres, architecture and painting are the ones that have flourished most, and they are unquestionably the ones that have

achieved the greatest international fame. The very considerable achievements in other cultural domains, such as learning and music, have been confined to a greater extent within the nation's borders. That such great poets and prosaists as Vondel, Hooft and Huygens are so little known beyond the country's borders is due to the smallness of the Dutch language area. There is no doubt at all that

295 Many houses along Amsterdam's canals are still embellished by grisailles, known as 'Witjes' after Jacob de Wit, who excelled in this 18th century variant of the trompe l'oeil. The work, entitled 'Autumn', undoubtedly hung in the usual place next to a window, where it caught a lot of light. 296 'Isaac blesses Jacob' by Govert Flinck, a pupil of Rembrandt and one of the Amsterdam masters of the 17th century.

the others, the most notable are the Stedelijk Museum, the Vincent van Gogh Museum, the Amsterdam Historical Museum and the Tropical Museum. The first of these chiefly contains post-1850 art; the core of the Vincent van Gogh Museum is its large collection of Van Gogh's works but the

296

297

they would have played a greater part in the world of literature if they had written in a language that was more widely spoken. Hugo de Groot, better known outside The Netherlands under the Latinized form of his name, Hugo Grotius, had much less difficulty crossing national frontiers because his famous work 'De Jure Belli ac Pacis' (On the Law of War and Peace) was written in Latin. With this book Grotius laid the foundations of modern international law.

The painter's art does not suffer from the same limitations as the writer's in this respect, and it is therefore painting above all which has become the symbol of the blossoming of culture in the 17th century. The florescence of painting gave the Netherlands pride of place alongside Italy. Explanations for this pheno- menon have often been sought. Ac- cording to Professor J.J.M. Timmers, in his 'Dutch Life and Culture', the basic reason lies in the remarkable

sense of realism which is characte- ristic of the inhabitants of the Low Countries and stands in sharp con- trast to the rationalism and decorative sense of the Italians. This realism is already to be seen in the works of the painters of the 15th and 16th centuries, who by preference placed their figures in a faithfully rendered interior, city- scape or landscape. Religious themes had less chance in the Republic than in Italy, and the Dutch painters there- fore directed their attention rather to landscapes, seascapes, cityscapes and interiors, all of them themes in which light was a dominant element. Another genre to be carried to great heights was portraiture. Frans Hals' work reaches its culmination in his portraits, in which, as in those of Rembrandt, light played a magical part. The portrayal of daily life was another favourite genre, and Jan Steen, Van Ostade and Adriaen Brouwer in

297 Genre piece by Willem Buytewech: 'Merry Company'. 298 'The Banquet of the Civic Guard' by Bartholomeus van der Helst, 1648. The banquet was held at the crossbow range on the Singel to celebrate the Peace of Westphalia. 299 A typical scene from 18th century Amsterdam: 'The Bookshop of Pieters Meijer Warnars' by J. Jelgerhuis.

298

particular excelled in it. The chief patrons were not, as in other countries, monarchs and men of similar distinction but the well-to-do citizenry. Aside from buying paintings, these prosperous members of Dutch society liked to have portraits made of themselves. This propensity gave rise to a new genre, native to the Republic, namely the group portrait. Within the genre the most notable works were those portraying civic guards and governors. This is the great genre of Dutch painting, reaching its apogee in Rembrandt's 'Nightwatch' and 'Staalmeesters' ('The Sampling Officers of the Drapers' Guild'), in Frans Hals' portraits of civic guards, governors and governesses and in Van der Helst's civic guard pieces. As the great majority of the works remained within the borders, it is only in The Netherlands, and particularly in Amsterdam, that they can be seen and admired. The Golden Age lasted for only a relatively short space of time: from the first decade of the 17th century roughly to the year of disaster 1672, which must be regarded as a turning-point. This was the year in which the wars with France, England and German bishops to the east caused trade to wither and – as legend has it – grass to grow in what at other times were the bustling streets of Amsterdam.

After this turning-point, the indigenous Dutch culture began to lose ground to the fashions imported from France. The result was a hybrid, which was to characterize the 18th century in particular. In Dutch history the 18th century is treated as a slow and dull age. Nevertheless, for the country's cultural life it was a period of uninterrupted vitality. Science, belles lettres and domestic architecture attained hitherto unknown heights. Painting managed more or less to hold its own for a time but finally deteriorated into a purely national school lacking a wider appeal. Gone then for ever was the Golden Age, the age that shaped the city as we know it today, the Amsterdam that this book has endeavoured to explore.

Amsterdam, 'gezellige stad'

The most charming of all the songs about Amsterdam opens with the words 'On Amsterdam's canals...', and whether it is a boisterous song in which everybody joins in or one quietly to be listened to, ever and again the Westertoren rises up as a reassuring and dependable father figure. When songs about Amsterdam are rendered in the style of the old working-class district the Jordaan, the notes are always romantically drawn out, the accordionist sounding long and sonorous chords while the singer makes the large gestures of a dramatic tenor with his arms. Amsterdam might also on occasion be made fun of, criticized or lamented, depending on the circumstances, but unsung it will never be. Anyone with anything to say will always find a platform and an audience; the name 'Amsterdam' has magic, it stirs profound emotions.

The singers of the Jordaan use the old dialect of the city, in which all the vowels are so distorted that they become dark tones and consonants are hissed at the most unexpected moments. To the Jordaans dialect the Jewish community, which accounted for 10% of the pre-war population and was just as deeply rooted in 'Mokum' (the originally Jewish nickname for Amsterdam), added its own intonation and vocabulary. Outsiders may have difficulty with the resultant mixture, but the sharp ear of a connoisseur would have been able to discern many more variants in the city's heyday. Almost every district had its own nuances and one such variant, Hooghaarlemmerdijks, still survives in affected speech.

Jordaans is Amsterdam's warm and unpretentious language. Those using it can say things in a homelier way, with more feeling and subtler shades of meaning. For generations Jordaans was the language used by all comedians. It also crops up unexpectedly in other circles, for example among artists, who have instinctively adopted the speech of the ordinary people as an alternative to Received Standard, which they consider too formal, cold and middle-class.

The Westertoren stands precisely at the dividing line between the crescent of canals and the old Jordaan. The Jordaner celebrates it in song as the faithful watchman standing guard at the end of every narrow street, but that is about all. For the rest he prefers the homely atmosphere of Aunt Leen's or Uncle Dirk's pub, where life is pleasant and snug. Other singers bring in the canals that sweep in wide concentric arcs around the medieval heart of the city, enclosing it so securely that it becomes a nest, a world apart, or – as the poets are found of saying – a womb, warm and fertile.

Whatever other criticisms outsiders may have of Amsterdam nobody denies that it is a friendly, sociable city. Its genial, anti-authoritarian, rather forward nature makes it a city in which it is easy to feel at home. When the great urban centres began to languish in the late 1950s as a result of the explosive growth of traffic and the migration of the middle classes to suburbia, Amsterdam was the only city in Holland that preserved its function as a meeting place. The result was that in the 1960s all of Holland's rebellious youth, as well as contingents from other countries, assembled in the heart of the old city to embark on a festival of renewal that was to go down in history as the Provo movement. These explosive puberty rites have played their part in making Amsterdam what it is today. Provo has become embedded in the Amsterdam mentality, or, rather, the old revolutionary and republican spirit of Amsterdam has found expression in Provo and made itself heard in an increasingly utilitarian and bourgeois age.

Just as Amsterdammers found it entirely natural that the inner city should be kept free of tall, concrete

office blocks, that canals should remain canals and that radical changes
should be avoided, so too they wanted
to defend their freedom of speech
and action against 'the authorities',
whoever they might be. Governing
Amsterdam is something like running
the gauntlet. Anyone who would try it
must be prepared for unexpected
outbreaks of opposition; more impor-
tantly, he must be fully alive to the
fact that this is a city in which power
has to be exercised with a good deal of
caution, wisdom and humour.
If at all possible Amsterdammers
want to have the best of both worlds.
They have got it into their heads that
barrel organs are a traditional part of
the city's ambience. Don't ask them
why; it just is so. And therefore it is
up to the authorities to make sure

*300 One of the many drawbridges
which still exist in Amsterdam: where
the river Amstel and the Nieuwe Herengracht flow together. 301 Houseboat on
the river Amstel giving a good impression of the special atmosphere.*

that barrel organs can be seen and
heard, preferably in the busiest parts
of town where traffic has a job to keep
moving. Let him who dares try to get
rid of a herring stall, pull down an old
church or touch a cultural institution:
protests will come thick and fast, and
since Provo these have taken on
ingenious forms.
A conservative city concerned with
preserving whatever is of value – and
Amsterdam, with its rich history, is
bristling with fascinating relics. At
the same time, a city with a craving
for the new – inquisitive, fashion-
conscious, internationally oriented
and always ready to welcome the
unusual.
Because of this, anyone taking a walk
in the city to look, shop and enjoy
himself has a wide range of choices.
It's all there, all interwoven. A big
city, a capital, but unmistakably
Amsterdam. For the foreign visitor,
above all this means intimate,
graceful, painstaking, nowhere the
din of broad boulevards that lead to
monumental edifices, to residential

buildings doing their best to look like
palaces, or shops and hotels catering
to the need for ostentation. Amsterdam is very Dutch in its tendency to
keep things down to normal proportions. A city of details, a city for
strollers, nowhere dull, full of variety.
The Dam is the centre of the web.
From there, shopping streets go in all
directions, each of them with a different character determined by the
districts to which they lead. The most
expensive thread travels south, to the
Leidseplein and beyond, through the
P.C. Hooftstraat to the Concertgebouw, the museum district. A
thread of working-class establishments runs west via the Nieuwendijk
and the Haarlemmerdijk. And each of
them has its own special attractions.
Between these radii stretch the
canals, still, and increasingly, unique
high-quality residential areas. And for
the stroller a breathtaking experience,
for it is here that Amsterdam unfolds
an almost endless succession of old
houses, without shops or places of
entertainment, peaceful yet festive.

301

On the Singel near the Munt is the floating flower market, the last of the many markets which were held on the canals in former days. It is always crowded and, with the old Munt Tower in the background, presents as merry a scene as one could wish.

Markets are to be found in every district throughout the length and breadth of the city, but for devotees two of them are rather special.

The first is the Waterlooplein market, which was once the central market of the old Jewish quarter, and in fact of the entire city, because all that Amsterdam yielded in the form of discarded possessions, everything that the rag-and-bone men collected on their daily rounds, turned up again here for sale. When there is something an Amsterdammer does not like or want any more he will say: Take that to the Waterlooplein. And he himself will probably be among those who visit Waterloo Square in the hope of finding a bargain or discovering a work of art. After the toll taken of the Jewish population by the war, the market appeared to be doomed. However, it recovered and took on a new lease of life when the younger generation was struck by a sudden fancy

for dresses like grandmother used to wear and all the other things of which their parents had said: Take that to the Waterlooplein.

Of the local markets, the one that has most successfully turned itself into a major shopping centre is the Albert Cuyp market, situated in the Pijp. The Pijp (Pipe), a large, densely-populated, working-class district bordering the Amstel, has a high percentage of families of foreign extraction, a large proportion of these being the families of the migrant workers known as 'guest workers'. Almost effortlessly the market has taken on a new rôle as a shopping and meeting place for these new Amsterdammers, who have still not forgotten their native cuisine and are to be seen at stalls with exotic products discussing, bargaining and handling and examining the wares as they were accustomed to do in their own countries.

Meanwhile, the market has surrounded itself with a large assortment of shops that cater primarily to the new inhabitants but also tempt the older inhabitants from time to time. The most important thing, however, is that the immigrant workers are beginning to feel at home in the Pijp

and are undergoing a transformation from outsiders to Amsterdammers with their own 'circuit' – though for the city's older inhabitants it can be something of a shock to hear one second-generation boy or girl addressing another in authentic Jordaans. The process of assimilation of quietly continues and the market acts as one of its catalysts.

A visit to the 'Albert Cuyp' is a must for anyone who wants to get to know the real Amsterdam of today. It is not on the tourist routes; it isn't beautiful, but it is certainly authentic.

Cinemas in abundance in Amsterdam, despite the competition from television. There is a sufficient body of discerning cinema-goers to ensure that the important films come to Amsterdam and stay there for a while. However, the visitor who would also like a taste of the cinema culture of yesteryear should certainly not miss the Tuschinski on the Reguliers-breestraat. It is unique in Holland. In the days when cinema made the tradition from fairground entertainment held in a tent to an established form of popular entertainment in the cities, fate decreed that a Polish Jew on his way as an emigrant to the New World should be delayed in Holland long enough to realize the potential that lay in this development. With the flair of a great showman Abraham Tuschinski built a cinema palace in the heart of Amsterdam that was to weather all storms.

While in other cities one cinema after the other is being pulled down, converted to provide multi-level parking or mutilated beyond recognition, Tuschinski has not only stayed in business but been painstakingly preserved in its original state by its owners. Even the exuberantly artistic carpets, reminiscent of the décors in

302 The daily refreshing of the water in the canals of Amsterdam enables the fishes to live and the fishermen to catch them. 303 Living on a houseboat might be pleasant but is not always easy. 304 (overleaf) Amsterdams boisterous harbour-life was recalled during the Sail manifestations in 1975 and 1980.

the old Fritz Lang films, are rewoven whenever bald patches begin to appear. On the opposite side of the street is a cinema that has an entirely different class of enthusiasts. Also of pre-war vintage, the Cineac was designed by the architect Duiker and, in contrast to the voluptuous approach taken to the Tuschinski, was intended to be simply an efficient 'newsreel machine'. The proponents of the new architecture jealously watch over the Cineac as a monument to their revolutionary early years.

There is no shortage of theatres either in Amsterdam. In the Provo period clashes occurred between the supporters of the old and the new, the issue being the types of works that should be staged in Amsterdam's principal theatre, the Stadsschouwburg (City Theatre) on the Leidseplein. The tensions that gave rise to Operation Tomato have now virtually disappear-

ed. The Stadsschouwburg has retained its traditional repertoire, but experiments of all kinds are given their chance in the numerous small theatres which have since sprung up. The outstanding example is still the Mickery, which is housed in a converted cinema on the Rozengracht, in the heart of the Jordaan, and continues indefatigably to explore the frontiers of dramatic communication. Whereas formerly most productions were by English and American groups, nowadays the theatre also regularly presents Dutch works. A meeting place for modern-theatre lovers, international in character and typical of a city for which English is a second mother tongue. Dutch through and through is the Werktheater on the Kattegat. Here one finds a new type of actors who make a serious study of the problems dealt with and develop their performances collectively – an approach

that is as difficult as it is fascinating and often produces highly praiseworthy results. Among the other distinctive theatres in Amsterdam are: De Krakeling on the Nieuwe Passeerdersstraat, which specializes wholly in theatre for children; the Soeterijn in the Linnaeusstraat, where the Third World can make itself heard; and the Balie on the Kleine-Gartmanplantsoen.

The way in which the last of these originated is typical of post-Provo Amsterdam. Among the buildings in the Leidseplein area, one of Amsterdam's main entertainment centres, was the House of Detention. The decision to close it down naturally aroused a great deal of interest among investors. There was opposition, however, to the idea of the site's being used for a hotel, an office block, a multi-storey car park or luxury flats. Through a combination of persistence

and ingenuity, the people who preferred to see the site more modestly used for theatres and other cultural facilities succeeded in attracting attention to themselves, alerted Amsterdammers to what was happening and invited the country's best architects to submit projects. The result was an impasse which afforded the opportunity for calm discussion. The empty building was hastily occupied by a number of institutions, and also a theatre, whose name De Balie (The Bar) was derived from the building's original function. This is one way of founding theatres and solving problems...

The same thing that happened to the Stadsschouwburg with Operation Tomato happened to another renowned and long-established institution, Het Concertgebouw (Concert Hall), with Operation Nutcracker. Here too the result was the emergence of all sorts of new musical centres, as diverse in nature as the music itself. Meanwhile, works by the Nutcrackers are already being performed in the Concertgebouw. Surprisingly enough, one classic institution from the days of Provo, the gaily coloured Paradiso on the Weteringschans, has managed to survive. Still good for a revolutionary happening, still much-debated and ever on the verge of collapse, the Paradiso may not be a place for the average citizen but it has securely established itself in the constellation of Amsterdam's most remarkable institutions. Revolutions everywhere except in the Stedelijk Museum (Municipal Museum), because this was one of the instigators of the revolution, the only established art institute that, far from avoiding the new, sought it out and cultivated it. The process of proliferation manifested itself in this area chiefly in the appearance of dozens of new art dealers. A list without end, extremely varied and a force to be reckoned with in the

306

artistic life of Amsterdam, where artists feel as much at home as civil servants do in The Hague. What impressed you most in Amsterdam? I asked a French friend. His answer surprised me: All the bric-à-brac shops, where you can find literally everything. 'The Historical Museum in the Kalverstraat,' an ageing American said in the train to Paris. 'One of the most modern museums I've ever seen.' Not a single person mentioned the red-light district and the whole sex scene, which is a thorn in the flesh to the average Amsterdammer but was allowed to mushroom in the tolerant '60s and '70s.

Much remains to be said still – about the museums, about the cafés, the eating-houses, cabarets, districts with a character all of their own, renovated churches, almshouses, restoration projects, the ever-expanding exhibition centre the RAI, the green cult, Schiphol, sightseeing boats, the old harbour districts, the converted warehouses, the two universities, the press, the publishing houses, the beautiful-people scene, red, Catholic, Protestant,

Jewish and liberal nostalgia, the big bookshops and antique shops, the brown pub cult, houseboats, post-Provo squatters, the Bijlmermeer suburb, the Amsterdam School, Berlage's South Amsterdam, Willink's houses, Vondelpark, the Floriade flower show, Hotel Americain, the garden suburbs, Ajax, the artists' society Arti, the plans for the new town hall, the Surinamers, Artis Zoo, etc. All of them things that have to do with Amsterdam as it moves down the years, chatting, debating, quarrelling, laughing and toiling, an old place where it has all been going on for a very long time, where every dream has left some trace behind and past mistakes can not always be remedied. Like Florence, Venice, Vienna and Toledo, Amsterdam lives with the memory of a mighty past to which it owes both its beauty and the nostalgia and ambition in its character. A past that oppresses and inspires, and a character that contains a remarkable mixture of conservatism and progressiveness. According to the experts on such matters, provided the two are

305 One of the attractions on the Dam Square is the feeding of the pigeons.
306 An attractive spot is the daily Flower Market along the Singel near the Koningsplein.

307

307-310 Around the Waag, the former St. Anthoniespoort on the Nieuwe Markt, a weekly busy market is held which specialises in a great variety of antiques from grandmothers days. It is the real fleemarket of Amsterdam.

present as a dualism in each individual rather than being separately represented by warring factions, these are the ideal ingredients for an urban culture.

The most compelling facets of the Amsterdam character are its tolerance, its unyielding opposition to discrimination and its dislike of vio-

308

309

lence. Provo turned the city upside down for a time and had international repercussions, but what the many foreign reporters who wrote about it never fully understood was that Provo encountered so little opposition from the citizenry because it was non-violent and humorous. Such violence as there was came from the autorities, who did not know what to do with the movement. The Provos themselves harmed nobody. If we can still speak about Amsterdam as a warm and friendly city in an age in which so many others have sacrificed their charm to traffic and commercial inte-rests, it is thanks to Provo, which recaptured Amsterdam for the ordi-nary citizen. The liveableness of a city is not merely a question of shopping and entertainment facilities and the beauties of the urban environment; it is also and above all the way the inhabitants approach their city, the familiarity of the terms on which they live with it. An Amsterdammer who removes a paving stone so that he can plant a tree in front of his house is committing an offence, but at the same time he is giving expression to a need for liveable surroundings; he wants more greenery in his street. The people Carmiggelt writes about in his daily column under the name Kronkel may not be the jolliest people imaginable, but at least they don't smother their feelings. Amsterdam-mers are communicative; asked or unasked, they say what they think and feel. Amsterdam is sometimes called the Low Countries' most southern city, though according to the experts it mainly has Frisian blood in its veins. As a result of the enormous growth of tourism and the sharp increase in the number of foreign inhabitants, the city has rapidly become internationalized. A new Amsterdam is emerging, one which on occasion draws despondent comments from the older generations of inhabitants because, once again, Amsterdam 'isn't what it used to be'. In fact, a process of swift assimilation is taking place and its results are

310

fascinating. As so often before in its long history, the 'womb' has once more become fertile. Recent developments symbolize this development, which will be a beneficial one as long as

Amsterdam continues to be generous and tolerant enough not to begrudge anyone a place in the sun. It always takes a bit of getting used to, but it has always worked. While the carillon high in the Westertoren peals out over the Jordaan and the neighbouring canals, a new song is being born in Amsterdam.

Lovely! say the people in the sightseeing boat. True, but there is more to the city than that. Much more. A friendly city, Amsterdam. Warm and vulnerable.

311 A merry goodbye from Amsterdam with a band marching on the square before the Noorderkerk along the Prinsengracht.

311

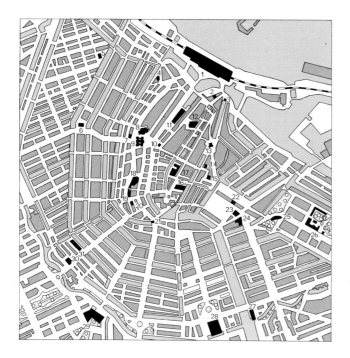

The old city of Amsterdam

1 Central Station, *2* St. Nicolas Church, *3* Schreierstoren (Tower of Tears), *4* Ronde Lutherse Kerk (The Domed Lutheran Church), *5* Noorderkerk (North Church) in the Jordaan, *6* Westerkerk (West Church), *7* Postoffice, *8* Nieuwe Kerk (New Church), *9* Paleis op de Dam (Royal Palace, former townhall), *10* World War II memorial, *11* Stock exchange, *12* Oude Kerk (Old Church), *13* Waag, Nieuwmarkt (Weighhouse, New Market), *14* Pinto-house, *15* Zuiderkerk (South Church), *16* Oudemanhuispoort (Old men's house gate), *17* Townhall, *18* Burgerweeshuis (City Orphanage, now Amsterdam Historical Museum), *19* Begijnhof, *20* Maagdenhuis, now University of Amsterdam, *21* Munt (Mint), *22* Mozes and Aäron Church, *23* Academy of Architecture, *24* Synagogues, *25* Hortus Botanicus (Botanical Garden), *26* Artis (Zoological Garden), *27* Amstelhotel, *28* Nederlandse Bank, *29* Rijksmuseum, *30* Stadsschouwburg (Theatre), *31* Paleis van Justitie (Palace of Justice).

Major Museums of Amsterdam

Name and address	Subject
Allard Pierson Museum Oude Turfmarkt 127 Tel.: 5252556	Rich archaeological collection
Museum Amstelkring 'Ons' Lieve Heer op Solder O.Z. Voorburgwal 40 Tel.: 246604	Clandestine church
Amsterdam Historisch Museum Kalverstraat 92 Tel.: 255822	History of Amsterdam
Anne Frankhuis Prinsengracht 263 Tel.: 279027	In memory of Anne Frank
Natura Artis Magistra Plantage Kerklaan 38-40 Tel.: 231836	Zoological Garden
Aviodome Schiphol Airport Tel.: 173640	National air and space travel museum
Bijbels Museum Herengracht 366 Tel.: 247949/242436	History of the Bible
Fodor Keizersgracht 609 Tel.: 249919	Modern art
Rijksmuseum Vincent van Gogh Paulus Potterstraat 2 Tel.: 764881	Vincent van Gogh and works of his contemporaries
Werf 't Kromhout Hooge Kadijk 147 Tel.: 250302	Steam dockyard
Museum van Loon Keizersgracht 672 Tel.: 245255	Old furnished canalhouse
Madame Tussaud Kalverstraat 156 Tel.: 229949	Panopticum
Geschiedkundig Medisch Pharmaceutisch Museum Waaggebouw, Nieuwmarkt 4 Tel.: 242209	Medical history
Nederlands Instituut voor Nijverheid en Techniek (NINT) Rozengracht 224 Tel.: 248168	Industry/technology
Nederlands Persmuseum Oude Hoogstraat 24 Tel.: 5253908	Press
Rembrandthuis Jodenbreestraat 4-6 Tel.: 249486	Most of Rembrandt's etchings
Rijksmuseum Stadhouderskade 42 Tel.: 732121	Dutch art 1500-1900
Nederlands Scheepvaartmuseum Kattenburgerplein 1 Tel.: 254175	Maritime history
Stedelijk Museum Paulus Potterstraat 13 Tel.: 732166	Modern art
Theatermuseum Herengracht 168 Tel.: 235104	Theatre
Tropenmuseum Linnaeusstraat 2 Tel.: 652680	Life and work in the tropics and sub-tropics
Museum Willet-Holthuysen Herengracht 605 Tel.: 264290	Patrician Mansion 1700
Paleis, Koninklijk Dam Tel.: 248698	Interior
Six Collectie* Amstel 218 Tel.: 266900	Dutch artists (Rembrandt, Frans Hals, etc.) in patrician mansion
Wijnkopersgildehuys Koestraat 10-12 Tel.: 231210	Vintner's guild house
Zoölogisch Museum Plantage Middenlaan 53 Tel.: 5223624/5222422	Zoology

* = on introduction by director of the Rijksmuseum only

Index

The numbers refer to the photographs